Ascension Messages
From the
Higher Realms

The Process of
Conscious Human Evolution

ASCENSION MESSAGES
FROM THE
HIGHER REALMS

The Process of
Conscious Human Evolution

WENDY ANN ZELLEA

New Era Edition

Happy Awareness Publications
Maywood, NJ

Ascension Messages From the Higher Realms – The Process of Conscious Human Evolution – New Era Edition

Copyright © 2019 Happy Awareness Publications

The author and publisher respectfully acknowledge that this book is copyrighted. No part of this publication may be reproduced in any form by any means without the written permission of the copyright holder.

This publication is distributed with the expressed and applied understanding that the author and publisher are not engaged in rendering professional advice. If professional advice or other expert assistance is required, the services of a competent professional should be sought.

Neither the author nor publisher makes any representation or warranty of any kind with regard to the information contained in the book. No liability shall be accepted for any actions caused by or alleged to be caused, directly or indirectly from using the information contained in this book.

This writing is channeled. This means that there is a particular vibration the way the words are written.

If you wish to share any of my writing, please do not change it.

In addition, please give credit where credit is due.

This is the work of Wendy Ann Zellea.

Library of Congress Control Number:2019950901

ISBN: 978-1-7321775-3-6

Wendy@AnEnlightenedAuthor.com

AscensionMessages.com

AnEnlightenedAuthor.com

*To my Soul Family.
It's all about Love!*

Contents

A Message from the Masters 1
Introduction 5

PART I 7

You Are What You Think 9
The Power of Words 17
Our Third Dimensional Selves 21
Truth, What We Choose to Believe 25
Re: Religion 29
Our Soul Family 37
Good Grief 43
Well-Being 53
Ancient Healing 65
The Weight of the World 69
Out With the Old 79
How to Waste Time 81
Recent World Events 85
Only the Good Stuff 89

PART II 93

I Stepped Off a Cliff and Didn't Fall 95
Really Happy 99
Trusting Ourselves 105
Be Here Now 113
Believe It 117
Self-Esteem 121
Success 127
Being Grateful 131
If I'm So Enlightened… 137

PART III 141

The Garden of Eden 143
Channeling the New Paradigm 149
The Higher Self 153

The Process of Ascension 159
Ascension Symptoms.. 161
Knowing 165
Celestial Events... 171
It's Time 177
A Divine Life... 181
Changing Our Past... 189
We Are Stars.. 193
Conscious Human Evolution 199
The Law of Attraction... 203
Synchronicity 207
The Mystery of Parallel Realities 209
Nothing... 213
Angels and Ascended Masters 219
New Wisdom 223
We are Our Own Spiritual Teachers 227
Observations of the Masters 231
Dimensions... 235
Know Thyself... 237
A Message from St. Germain... 239
About the Author 241
More Books by Wendy Ann Zellea..................................243

A Message from the Masters

The process of Conscious Human Evolution is happening, as both humans, and those of us in the Higher Realms, transition into The New Era. So, what is the next step, how do we go ahead, and what can we expect going forward?

That depends on each one of us. We are ready to help you claim your Divinity and bring forth your unique gifts into the world. Yes, there is a message lying dormant inside of us, waiting to be shared with those ready to hear it. We each have a purpose, destiny, reason for being here now.

How can we be sure of our path, as we go forward? We can, because the journey is the destination. We can begin by looking inward to find the guidance that has always been there. However, we, the Masters, are always here to assist. We are only waiting for you to ask.

Each of us knows what to do. A flower knows how to grow towards the light, and blossom at exactly the right time. An animal knows how to look for food and care for its young, so they can survive. When we were born, we did not doubt. We moved with perfect confidence, certain if we were hungry, sleepy, happy, or when it was time to cry.

We are here to guide, as *Living Beings*. Some of us have had a human experience, having to reconnect with our source of guidance and *knowing*. Now we are Masters.

However, because *you* have done the work, all of us are in The New Era, ascending higher and higher and changing how we experience ourselves and each other.

With this in mind, we will continue our journey, relying on our intuition and feelings to guide us, for we already have the intention to do so, and that is the ticket.

We are capable of successfully achieving our goals. We can measure our progress by looking back and remembering where we were years ago. We will see that there has been growth and there will continue to be.

The Ascension Process has no end. It is ongoing and eternally fantastic. As we continue our journey, we realize, at no particularly special moment, that life is good, gentle, abundant, and graceful, and that everything goes smoothly, without much effort, all because we are on the path.

This is the start of what might be the greatest event in human history. We, The Masters are part of it.

With much Love and Light,

The Masters through Wendy Ann Zellea

Introduction

If we could look at the smallest microscopic particle of matter within ourselves, we would see that there is still space surrounding it. We are all part of an infinite, ever-changing sea of atoms and molecules, suspended in nothingness.

In our day-to-day reality, at times we are not mindfully present, or focused on the moment. We plan future events and think of things that are not yet happening in our immediate surroundings. We flow in and out of moments of being completely in the *here and now*. Even though it is space that defines an object and gives it form, we tend to focus on objects, and not the space that surrounds them. When we begin to see both, we will experience the magic of life more fully.

Why are we here? The answer is that it is to experience life. If we set our intention to do so, we find that there is much more to *reality* than meets the eye. Beyond a thin veil, are many things we have yet to discover.

When we are willing to change, we pass out of the mundane. By moving from the mainstream flow of mass consciousness, and into the higher realms of higher energetic emanations, we can replace old ideas and beliefs with new ones. We then discover that we are Masters, taking part in the *Process of Conscious Human Evolution,* and fulfilling ancient agreements to hold the Light for humankind. There is no better time to begin the journey, because some of us already have.

Part I

Moving Out of the Collective Consciousness

You Are What You Think

Yes, it is true, our thoughts *do* create our reality. If we think life will go well, we will have a good chance of it being so. If we believe we are healthy and vibrant, we will be in the best position to be that way. When we criticize ourselves and others, we are ensuring the flow of an abundant supply of things to criticize. When we focus on the aspects of our lives for which we are grateful, we will continue to create the future we wish.

Monitoring our thoughts, making them positive and uplifting, is an ongoing process. This means slowing down and becoming aware of what we are thinking.

When we are living in the flow of the Collective Consciousness, our thoughts become entangled in the stream of what everyone else is thinking.

When we rise out of that vibration, we become consciously aware of ourselves and what we genuinely think and believe. It may be a challenge at first to change our thought processes, but as in everything else, the way to go ahead is to practice. We were not born with our old ideas, we learned them, and we can un-learn them and discover new ones.

When we pass through each day with an optimistic outlook, focusing on the *higher good*, we create balance, flow, and grace. Once we have improved our skills of positive thinking, we are ready for the next step.

Our thoughts create our reality.

Humanity is ascending to higher energetic levels. It may not appear so, when we look at world events, but at a higher-level there is progress, made by those who are raising their vibration exponentially.

We are moving out of the Collective Consciousness into a higher dimensional existence, by letting go of lower vibrating energies. This does not mean we are ascending into the clouds. Instead, we are creating new realities.

Imagine sitting in a beautiful room at home, where the lights are low, there is soft music playing, you are wearing comfortable flowing clothes, you have not a care in the world, and there is free time to stay and enjoy the calm surroundings. You can begin to create such a place in a higher dimension, in The New Era.

Suppose this experience was a regular part of your daily life, and the time you spend in this room, relaxing or even meditating, was the most cherished part of your day. Then visualize leaving the room and staying in that peaceful state of mind throughout the day, even while you sleep. You have stepped out of the Collective Consciousness and into a higher level of awareness. You are still right here on Earth, but your vibration is different. You have passed through the thinnest of veils, arriving into a new energetic place and leaving lower vibrating energies behind.

The Process of Conscious Human Evolution is cyclical. We tend to begin the early part of our journey with elementary energetic techniques, then move on to more esoteric ones. It can be beneficial to revisit these basic processes periodically, because deep-seeded energy can remain hidden, and re-surface as we transmute other issues. There is a sequence to the Ascension Process, which may be beyond our understanding, but we are able, using various methods, to identify areas in our Light bodies that still require clearing.

As we achieve higher levels of consciousness, it is important to remember that residual, lower, denser energies created in this lifetime, or brought with us from other incarnations, may be lingering in our Light Body.

We are multi-dimensional beings, simultaneously existing in other incarnations, levels of consciousness, and realms, and we can be affected by our connection to these aspects of ourselves. Therefore, we can maintain the vibrational integrity in our Third Dimensional existence, by releasing these lower discordant energies. Intention is a powerful ally, and we can use it to become conscious of energy that feels heavy to us, and then release it.

Moving out of our own way.

Being aware of the kind of dialogue we have with ourselves, is essential in the Process of Conscious Human Evolution. Many of us understand logically, that it is better to remain positive, but being positive on an intellectual level, is different from being so on a multi-dimensional one, where we must consider what we are *really* thinking.

If we decide to look for a new job, do we say to ourselves, *Oh, I won't get one anyway, there aren't any jobs out there, or the economy is bad*. We only need *one* job, and it might be just out there waiting for us.

When it comes to the economy, it is always going to fluctuate and self-regulate, so it does not make sense for us to accept the mass thought form that the economy is weak or strong. If we go through our lives seeing the possible scarcity that may exist, even when we are prospering, how can we ever hope to recognize the abundance that is already in our lives.

Abundance is not a measure of our bank balance, instead it is a feeling that we have when we experience the bliss and security of knowing there is trust in life. Those of us that are in a stream of abundance and prosperity, embrace it as it flows into our lives on a regular basis.

I was not always conscious of my ability to experience abundance. There was a time in my life, when I lived in a village in a Third World country. I had very few possessions, including no electricity or running water, and little income. Even then, I did not despair, for I always believed life would support me, and it did, although in those days it was on a much smaller scale.

I lived in Belize for fifteen years, and during that time I began to realize that everything occurs in a perfectly orchestrated fashion. I had a tiny shop in my home, where I created and sold hand painted t-shirts. In the slow tourist season, I always magically made a sale just when I thought the money would run out, allowing me to feel sincere gratitude on many occasions.

I was born in New Jersey but chose to live on an island in the Caribbean. It was an easy choice, and the opportunity for personal growth was one I might not have experienced otherwise. Being a foreigner, something I had not experienced in the United States, was an *eye-opener*.

The local inhabitants had ways of thinking that were different than what I was used to, and many were rather refreshing. Life on the island was relaxing. There is rhythm in the dialect of the locals, and grace and flow in their movement.

The day's activities took place primarily outdoors, we walked barefoot on the Earth, ate the food that grew locally, and the fish we caught from the sea. It was not a perfect life, many of the usual, everyday issues existed, but for me it was new and interesting.

I was fortunate enough to arrive on the island of Caye Caulker in 1986, when it was still relatively unaffected by American culture. There was no TV and only one phone. Occasionally someone would call the island phone office. If the call was for someone living nearby, one person would yell out the window to their neighbor, who would call to the next one, and so on until the recipient of the call heard there was a phone call for them.

There were very few vehicles on the small island, which was one mile by three blocks, so everyone walked barefoot on the soft, sandy streets. It was truly a little paradise. We cooked three times a day, ate fresh fish, and drank rainwater collected in wooden vats in the yard. We went to sleep early and woke up early. A few tourists came, but the men mostly fished or kept lobster traps and the women stayed at home. Some made local food, which their children brought around to sell.

I learned to cook the island food, including a wide variety of lobster dishes, such as lobster pasta, soup, and delicious lobster salad. Some people salted the lobster, dried it on the tin roof in the sun and then pan-fried it up for breakfast. It tasted like bacon. On the opening day of lobster season, many friends came by with a pound of lobster tails as a gift.

Those were the days...

The Power of Words

Every culture has its *sayings*, expressions intended to communicate a sort of wisdom for different situations. For example, if you convey advice to another person, and they do not follow it, you might say, *you can lead a horse to water, but you can't make him drink*.

Colloquialisms change, new expressions become fashionable, while others fade away. Most of these phrases appear to be harmless little anecdotes, but some are the means by which we sabotage ourselves without even realizing it.

One such phrase, which I hear all too often is, *it's always something*. It refers to an unexpected or undesirable event that we wish did not happen. It is not *always something*. If it were, then life would be a constant stream of mishaps and we would only notice when things went well. In addition, it is an affirmation that we are powerless over what happens in our lives.

Knowing it is *not always something*, liberates us from the mindset that we are walking potential victims, just waiting for something to go wrong.

Speaking impeccably...

Another frequently used ditty is, *with my luck*. There is no such thing as luck. Rather, there are events that happen as a result of the intentions that we create and send out into the Universe. When life goes well, it is because we expect the best outcome and believe in progress and success, rather than failure and unfortunate circumstances.

By uttering, *with my luck*, we are allowing life to send us, what we consider to be unlucky events. making ourselves into hapless victims and welcoming in circumstances we do not want.

From our *word*, comes what we create. If we desire something in life, it does not make sense to say that it will not happen, because then we are focusing on it not happening, and perhaps even making it more difficult to manifest. If we wish to have changes in our life, we should not say that we cannot have them, or we will find that we will be standing in our own way.

When something wonderful happens, if we say, *I don't believe it*, we are diminishing it. When synchronistic events occur, we can be happy and accept them wholeheartedly. When we wish to create something, we can begin by visualizing that it has already happened.

Any goal must first be an intention.

A few years ago, after I discovered I was living in a flood plain, I decided it was time to move to a new apartment. I made a mental list of the features I required in my new home. The unit would ideally be on the third or fourth floor, have a balcony, and a dishwasher.

I looked at all the possible rentals in the area and left my name with the management offices of the ones I was considering. Just at the perfect time, I got a call from my first choice, saying that there was an apartment on the fourth floor with a balcony and a dishwasher. The apartment was large, the rent was reasonable, and here I sit, listening to the dishwasher doing its job as I write.

It is not just that I am lucky, but I expect my life to move forward seamlessly, by imagining the best outcome. In addition, and this is essential, I take all the necessary steps I can at the time, to achieve my goal. And I give thanks when it all works out the way I hoped it would, or even better.

Our Third Dimensional Selves

When we want to say *no*, we can feel free to say it, and when we want to say *yes*, we can do that too. We have a responsibility to ourselves to set our own boundaries. Of course, there are many ways to say the same thing, but what is essential is to be honest with ourselves about what we truly desire.

When we were young children, we said *yes* and *no* without hesitation. Saying *yes* did not cause too much trouble, but as soon as we learned to say *no*, we ardently began to state our objections to limitations that were placed on us.

How wonderful we felt when we discovered we could say *no*. The world was ours. Everything was going to be our way, exactly as we wished. What could be better? All our little lives, people had been telling us *no*, and now we had joined the *no* club and could say *no*. However, our joy was short-lived. We obeyed others when they said *no*, but we did not achieve the same result when we said it back. In fact, quite the opposite happened.

When we said *no*, our mother and father got angry. We might have tried a few more times, but after a while we stopped. That was when we became disconnected from our feelings. We could not say *no*, so why bother? We began to do what others wanted us to do, not what WE wanted. After a while we stopped even thinking about what we truly desired, no less trying to achieve it.

Then came the teenage years, when our desires began to re-surface, and the choice was before us to continue to either do what our parents and the world expected of us, to follow our friends, or to do what we felt like doing.

Most of us go a little wild as teenagers, the degree being determined by how repressed we have been, and our individual personalities. It is the time of our lives when we can either become unique beings or follow the crowd. Those of us who choose individuality will be loners. Those who follow others will have the good opinion of their peers and their family.

However, the rewards of approval become diminished when we begin to lose ourselves in the crowd. On the other hand, the loneliness of those who choose to go their own way is lessened by the feelings of fulfillment that being connected to one's self affords.

It is our task as adults to create our own beliefs. We learn the ideas of our parents and teachers when we are children, and when we approach adulthood, we begin to create our own truth. The teenage years are the testing grounds, and the years following are the proving grounds.

Speaking our truth.

When we get to the root of what really makes us happy, we are moving with the Rhythm of Life. Suppose we do not want to go to work, should we quit our job and just take our happiness to the grocery store? Not if we like the paycheck we receive and the living it provides us. I do. So why would any of us want to quit our job and have no money? Most of us would not even know what to do with our time if we left our job, even if we still had plenty of money.

The important thing is to decide whether we do not want to work, or instead that we want to work at something we love. My goal was to work at what I loved. I was able to leave one job and start a new career that I enjoyed much more, one that also allowed me to support the standard of living I set for myself.

As we begin to evaluate what we would like for our lives, we can always ask for guidance. Whom should we ask? We can ask who we think we should ask. We can ask life, or the universe, or ourselves, the main thing is to ask. Angels and Ascended Masters are waiting to help us, but they cannot unless we request their help. If we never try, we will never know.

Truth, What We Choose to Believe

Whatever we believe to be true, is true. An entire planet of people may accept an idea, and it becomes a collective reality. However, if one person does not consider that thought to be true, then is it still absolutely true?

Over time, people began to believe that men were superior to women, we must grow old, that the New Year begins on January 1st, and the list goes on and on. Many of these ideas came about at the same time across the planet, within groups of people who had no contact with each other.

Societies that consider themselves advanced, view those who have held on to their old ways, as backward. They do not remember that at one time they were the same.

In the future, there will be those who look at us as antiquated. Perhaps one day, children will read about the Dark Ages where people sucked the blood of the

Earth in the form of oil, causing the planet and its inhabitants to become sickly. To those forthcoming civilizations, who have learned to use technology to create a clean, healthy environment for all, we will appear uncivilized.

There was a time when people thought the Earth was flat, a concept most of us find inconceivable. Quantum Physicists are now discovering that a theory such as Dualism, which has been the fundamental basis of modern physics for centuries, is not necessarily valid.

We are not separate from everything in the world. We are part of it. It does no good to look upon past beliefs as backward, because they were steppingstones to more evolved ways of thinking, each one being essential to get where we are now. We can be thankful for our progress and the lessons we learned.

Currently, with the help of sonar and satellite technology, there are scientists and archeologists that are uncovering proof that advanced human and extra-terrestrial societies existed on Earth more than 11,000 years ago and even much longer.

These discoveries. which have met the resistance from the traditional scientific community, will eventually require us to re-write human history and to accept that in spite of what we would like to believe, we are not the most advanced civilization that has ever existed here on Earth.

This is not the first time that the Collective Consciousness has been confronted with a new truth and been compelled to change its beliefs, and it will probably not be the last. Every culture supposes that they are more advanced than the generations that came before. It is the desire for newness and innovation, as opposed to being steeped in tradition, which will lead us to a better life in the future. It is the new frontier. I choose to be one of the pioneers.

Re: Religion

Religion is the act of living. When we come to realize that every step, and every breath we take, is a sacred act and each thought, word, or feeling is a prayer, life takes on new meaning.

Each of us is a spark of the divine and we should treat ourselves and others as such. The idea that God is an entity, separate from us, is a mass thought form that robs us of the divine aspect within each of us.

It is easy to control people who believe that God will punish them if they do not behave the way they are commanded, but when we truly believe that we are divine, there is no need for control because we Love, cherish and respect ourselves and others.

Much of humanity is convinced that their version of religion is the only true one. But as we transcend through the Process of Human Evolution, organized religion will not have a place in the truer spiritual experiences we embrace.

New belief systems will emerge over time. It is inevitable as humanity enters into the higher dimensions and becomes increasingly aware of the connection we have to one another and to the rest of the universe.

Some say that the tallest buildings in a society reflect the most important aspects of that culture. Ancient pyramids and temples were built in precise locations for specific reasons, such as to utilize powerful Earth energy spots, as transmission portals to communicate with civilizations in other planets and star systems, and as places of rejuvenation.

In the Middle Ages churches stood above all other structures, expressing that religion was the most important focal point of that time.

Currently, our skyscrapers mark an era in which money and commerce are the most highly regarded aspects of modern-day life, separating us from nature, the Earth, and the Universe.

However, an interesting development has magically occurred amid the materialistic frenzy that has been the prime-time activity of the developed world. A movement has been born and is rapidly spreading, people are consciously evolving.

This is the same evolution that Darwin spoke of, and it is happening as we speak. We are physically and energetically changing because of our environment and our beliefs.

Physical evolution takes place over prolonged periods of time; therefore, we do not see the gradual, outward changes as easily as we recognize the evolution of ideas, which change more rapidly.

What will happen to an entire generation of young people who spend most of their time texting and looking at the small screen on their cell phone? Some people criticize them for doing so, but from another point of view, they are developing new skills and diverse ways of approaching life. How that will manifest in the future we cannot know since it has not previously happened in our lifetime.

In the 1950's there was just as much criticism for those of us who talked on the phone for hours. People just do not like change. The telephone made the planet a smaller place, never to be the same, just as the world of cyber communication is doing.

We believe matter is static.

Human evolution has been taking place all along, throughout the years and over centuries, but it moves along at such a slow pace that we do not notice it. Think about the changes we have seen since the 1940's. We do not look like people did then, and it is not just their hair and make-up. It is a difference in the thoughts and feelings of that time, which we can see reflected in the demeanor of those in movies and in photographs.

I have seen people look much different after a Reiki class or other event that raised the vibration of those attending. Often a person comes to the class looking drained, and leaves looking vibrant, robust, and beautiful. Imagine how shifts in energy and belief systems can change appearances over longer periods of time.

There is a technique for looking at a person's aura, the energy body that surrounds the physical form. When the subject stands against a light-colored wall, in a room that is not too bright, and we squint and look at them, after a while we might see the color of their aura surrounding their physical body.

There are those who can do this naturally, just by looking at another person. In addition, after we watch a bit longer, the actual physical body of the person may change and their height, shape, and even the clothing can look different.

These changes happen all the time, but we do not see them because we believe matter is static. This is not necessarily so, our cells are constantly moving, living, dying, and reproducing. It is also possible to photograph the aura using Kirilian photography, and we can see the differences in the resulting photos.

Momentous changes are not far ahead and are happening in real time. All life resonates with the ingenious intelligence of the universe. As humans, we draw our power from the sacred geometry of creation and cyclical perfection of nature.

As we become more connected to this knowledge, our priorities will change. For example, when Autumn approaches, instead of following the TV schedule and the Fall Lineup of new shows and sporting events, we will look to the Autumnal Equinox and the phases of the moon to mark the season and our place in the Universe.

Organized religion uses the same corporate structure model as modern-day mega businesses. It acquired, or shall we say permanently borrowed, the original significant markers of natural cycles, changing them in order to celebrate, not the recurring events of our planet and universe, but rather what they deemed to be holy days that corresponded to the lives of the beings who were the focal point of their worship, such as Buddha or Jesus.

Coincidentally, these holy days all take place at similar times as the old marker days of natural cycles, but there was no mention of Earth, stars, or anything to do with the natural world. Those who continued to observe the cycles of nature, such as solstices, were branded as heathens, backward, or weirdoes.

It does not take long for a culture to change its beliefs on a mass scale, one or two generations can wipe the slate clean, and then we forget the old ways of thinking, even if they are still relevant.

After marking the passage of time artificially, with made-up calendars, *modern* cultures hardly remember the Earth's natural cycles. Oh yes, we pull out our summer fashions in May or June, packing them away again in September, but there is more significance to the changing of the seasons than wardrobe. For us to walk the path of true human beings, we must once again become connected to Cosmic cycles.

Organized religion has kept us away from this long enough. It was a good business model, made a lot of people a lot of money, but the time has come for a new plan. We cannot keep basing our lives on agendas that were invented hundreds of years ago, do not apply to us anymore, and do not produce the intended results.

The observance of the significant times of the year, including solstices and equinoxes, will bring us back to our natural rhythms, and closer to nature. We can return to the genuine human experience by connecting our energy with that of the planet upon which we live, the solar system of which we are a part, and the Universe that is the great mystery of life.

We do not need second-hand, watered down spirituality, doled out to us by those considered worthy of communing with heavenly beings. We are all inherently divine and can connect with the Divine within us.

The sages and Masters that walked the Earth came, not to be worshipped, but to show us our potential, so we could raise ourselves to higher levels of understanding, awareness, and enlightenment.

The powers that be did not want us to see our true human capabilities, for it was a threat to their job security, so they elevated the Masters to a state of divinity and convinced us that we could never, as mere humans, even dream of being like them, until we die of course. In the meantime, we can just pay them ten percent of our income, while they give us a bit of divine energy on a regular basis to keep us going, keep our spirits up, and keep us in line.

Organized religion still has its place in society, offering comfort and community to those taking part in it. It can also inspire. But as humanity moves forward, so must current traditional religion, if it is to remain the foundation of the spiritual belief systems of our culture. Praying includes admiring at a tree, the night sky, or the moon's waning and waxing. Listen to the birds and the crickets, they have messages for us. Doing so relaxes us and removes the stress of the day. When we stand on the Earth and feel the love of the planet vibrate through us, we heal and expand.

Our Soul Family

Children are young, intelligent human beings, whom we must nurture, Love, and guide. For them to learn respect, they must feel respected. When they feel valued, they will have self-esteem in adulthood.

Two-way communication is essential, allowing the child to express their desires. The parent can then rely on their wisdom to determine the best course of action in various situations. We can teach our beliefs to our children, but if we impose our ideas on them, forcing them to abandon their own, we lose their confidence and trust in us as they mature.

Some folks decide to have a baby to keep a relationship together or to prove how much they love one another person. It is not necessary for a couple to produce a child to have a happy or meaningful life together. We do not need children to work on the farm anymore, so with that in mind we might want to update our view of creating families.

Some women start to panic in their late thirties or early forties if they have not given birth. They create stress in their life and lower their sense of self-worth, by believing that to be a complete woman they must bear a child. It could be that they are not meant to be a parent, and their life may be destined to go in a different direction.

It is often deep-rooted in us that our sole purpose in life is to procreate, and that we are not whole unless it happens. Having a child because we believe we should, will not necessarily make us happy. However, if we truly wish to be a parent, then a child can bring us much joy.

Before bringing a child into the world, we should examine what our motivations are for doing so. Being a parent lasts a lifetime. Are we willing to devote the rest of our lives to a child? If the answer to that question is yes, then when that child is born it will be a blessed event. It gives us the opportunity to provide a loving, nurturing environment for another human being, allowing them to flourish and have a happy life.

Modern families are defined by love.

Relationships may not always be meant to last a lifetime, resulting in a new definition of the family unit.

A marriage that ends, is not necessarily unsuccessful. It just had an *expiration date*.

Human evolution is continuously occurring. We change more quickly than ever, and if the lines of communication do not remain open, we may find that the one we love has become a stranger and we cannot re-create the feelings we had in the beginning. When this happens, and we know the relationship has run its course, we can move on without guilt, sadness, or remorse, taking with us what we learned from the experience and the other person. We can see them as one of our teachers, hopefully the lessons were not too difficult.

In today's world we define modern families by both relationships as well as blood lines. If we live alone, *we* are our family of one. Even if we have siblings and parents who live somewhere else, in our own home we are the family unit.

The most important ingredient in the happiness or success of a family is not the housing arrangements, but the Love that exists among the members. It is possible for a parent to share more quality time with their children when they are not living with them, than when they are.

When families do not fit into the traditional category of mother/father/children, a family structure that is only one of many valid arrangements, we consider it broken or dysfunctional. A family does not need to fall apart just because the relationship of the parents has ended. It could be, that on some level, they only fell in love and married, or became a couple, because their children were meant to be born.

Reconnecting with our Soul family.

Alternatively, there is our soul family, those with whom we have traveled through many lifetimes and dimensions, pursuing similar goals. We can recognize members of our soul family because when we meet them, they seem familiar, as if we have known them before.

Those of us who have become consciously aware of our Soul families understand that on a higher level we are continuously and etherically connected. We tend to come together at significant times, such as celestial events and gatherings of like-minded people.

Soul family members come into our lives at significant personal times, as if orchestrated. They may be part of our biological family. We all know who we are and recognize one another by our vibration.

Whether a family includes traditional relatives, close friends, or Soul family members, those involved know who a part of the family is truly. Even if you are the only member, cherish your family and the family of humanity, to which we all belong.

Good Grief

Many of us will experience some form of grief in our lives, due to the loss of someone dear to us, but it is helpful to remember that grieving is a process, not a permanent condition. Grief is the energetic and emotional withdrawal that occurs in our Light Body when the vibration and resonance of a person who is no longer here, is removed from our Third Dimensional reality.

We normally experience profound energy shifts during the permanent physical separation from someone close, particularly when we have experienced their presence for all our lives.

In some societies, after a person dies there is a night of dancing, storytelling, card playing, and music. The purpose of the night of celebration is to drive away the grief, and it works, for that night at least.

In our culture, we tend to hold on to our feelings, many times to somehow hold on to the person.

Understanding the grieving process is easier when we can broaden our views about dying.

I lost both my parents within six months of one another. My father passed away suddenly in July 2008. The shock of losing him, my closest and dearest friend, was tremendous. With whom would I exchange current ideas, and talk about the books that we both read? Who would think so highly of me and praise my accomplishments?

My father was one of the wisest human beings I have ever known. His eighty-six years were filled with wonder, stimulating his curiosity, and driving him to pursue new frontiers and unknown realms of consciousness.

He taught me his standard of decency, respect for one's self and others, and most importantly to not ever go below my standard. My father was always there for me and loved me unconditionally, even when it seemed as though I was not entirely there for myself.

The joy I have is that I was able to contribute so much to his later years. Quite often he told me that I changed his life and opened new doors for him, even when he was eighty years old.

His mind was young, and he never ceased to think about possibilities, expressing wisdom that superseded that of most people I have ever known or read about. What a joy to know someone with whom I could share such mutual high regard. It was a gift and a magical experience in my life.

The most delightful moments were when I brought him a metaphysical book that he had not yet read. He would open it at once and start examining a few lines just to get a tidbit of what might be inside. When his eyesight began to decline, I bought him a full-spectrum lamp, and once again he was able to read his precious books, the window to the exciting frontier just ahead. I genuinely loved my father and if my life were only to have known him, I would say it was blessed. He was my Light and my anchor, my father, Martin William Zellea, 1922-2008.

My mother did not leave this world as quickly, but by early January 2009 she was gone. Even though it became clear that she would be gone close to the New Year, when it actually happened, it was as if I had never known at all.

My mother and I became very spiritually connected towards the end of her life. On a few occasions, while confined to a bed, I told her about everyday events that I had experienced, and she discussed them as if she had been there. I became aware that on some level she had also been present and was already beginning to experience her ability to be somewhere outside of her body, on a non-physical level.

She knew when I sent her Distance Reiki, pinpointing the exact time. My mother influenced many lives, and more than one person expressed to me that they would not be here today if it were not for her.

About a year before she passed, she told me quite casually during lunch one day that she always believed in me. I know that her Love was the blessing and grace that protected me and kept me returning to the right path throughout my life, even when it seemed as though I had become lost. She had a wonderful sense of humor, which I like to think she passed on to me. She was my teacher, my mother, Selma Grace Baratta 1926-2009.

The emotions that remained after she was gone were conflicting, and I had to sort them out. I missed her, but I was happy she was no longer suffering. I spent many hours in the hospital and gave her Reiki each time I visited, placing my hands on her legs while I sat beside the bed. I wanted to do everything I could to make her as comfortable as possible, but afterwards I was thankful I did not have to go there anymore and be in that depressing environment.

I did not allow myself to be guilty for feeling that way. Instead, I accepted that these emotions were not a measure of how much Love I had for my mother, but how much Love I have for myself. My honesty about my sentiments made it easier for me to experience the grieving process.

Celebrate the lives of those who depart.

For three days after my mother passed, I worked on creating a photo slide-show DVD for her memorial service. This distracted me from my emotions, but after the funeral I was confronted with the process that lie before me. My mother's death fell even heavier on top of the loss of my father, which was still in its own process. I began to feel drained. My usual happy, joyful self was gone.

One night as I sat at home, I thought to myself, *I don't want to feel like this anymore*. I knew my mother and father would not want me to despair either. It was then that I began to evaluate the grieving process, and by doing so I began to see the act of dying in a different light.

Let me begin by saying that I am not completely convinced that we are meant to die. It is an almost universal belief that we are, but I often wonder if ages ago, when humanity descended to a certain vibrational level, physical death became part of the cycle of life. At that point we forgot that when we existed at a higher vibration, we only transformed and ascended, taking our physical form with us.

However, since we are working in the framework of material life and death, I will only venture to say that once the dying process begins, our energy transforms so that we can move on. As that happens, the rest of us wishes to follow so that we can be whole again. As our Life Force Energy transitions to its next destination, we become less alive in the Third Dimension.

Some people leave suddenly, and others take longer, but it is all by design, because we live in a perfect universe. Therefore, it is a futile exercise for those of us who are still here, to wonder what we could have done differently or how a life might have been extended. When it is time for us to leave this world, we do, and our Higher Self will create whatever circumstances are necessary to achieve this departure.

We are always with the ones we love.

We might compare how we leave our life, to how different people enter the ocean to swim. Some run and jump and some wade in, gradually becoming accustomed to the water.

We assume that the physical condition of a person is what causes the person to pass, but we may have it backwards. If the etheric part of the person leaves the body first, the physical body expires, not able to continue without Life Force Energy. Similarly, a long-term illness is the result of the body reacting to the person's essence slowly leaving the physical form.

When a person is ill, and it is not time for them to go, the Life Force Energy returns, and they recover. If it is time to leave this incarnation, there is no physical healing, although there very well might be healing on other levels.

We do not have to look upon dying as something unnatural or untimely, for we all made agreements and contracts before we were born. In addition, we do not really die. We *continue on*, as Living Beings, instead of Human Beings, completing the incarnations we came to experience.

This is not just an exercise in semantics, nothing truly dies, because everything is made up of energy, which cannot be destroyed, only transformed and transmuted into something else. Those we love are always with us, and not just in our memories.

Currently we are evolving into higher vibrating energies, so now it is time to take another view of the processes of life. Some of us will die and others may ascend or pass into another reality, with bodies intact. Someday dying may be a very unusual occurrence.

In our daily lives, many of us do not experience births and deaths first-hand. Because of this, we are not accustomed to death as a part of the cycle of life. Death is not a tragedy, but an occasion to celebrate the life of a person and revere the process of the transition. We shall miss them, sometimes terribly, but on the other hand we can remember the time we had with them and know that in other places, we are still together.

We can Embrace the Love we shared with those that have gone, the Love that is real, and the Love that endures eternally.

> *Without all time and space,*
> *we're together face to face ...* George Harrison

The weekend after my mother passed, my Reiki teacher e-mailed me to let me know that she had taught a Reiki II class which included sending Distance Reiki. She asked her students to send Reiki to my situation and afterwards she wrote the following:

What I saw for you was how much you are at peace...not upset...a calmness from within. I saw your Mom and Dad "playing" around you... they get along very well on the other side...very playful and very much right around you. Your Father is on your right and your Mom on your left. When I sent Reiki to your spiritual body, it was beautiful. I saw your beautiful spirit...glowing and very full.

Two weeks later I took an astrology class and when the teacher read my chart, she mentioned that my mother left at a very auspicious time. I found this very comforting and quite interesting, because during the last days of my mother's life she told me that she kept thinking about my father, even though they had separated fifty years earlier, when I was seven years old.

My father once told me; *a man always loves his first wife*. I began to realize that when we have a connection with someone on one level, even if we do not spend our entire life with them, the connection can remain, often just as strong, if not stronger.

Going through my parent's possessions, I found that each of them had a small glass bird. Both birds now reside on a table in front of my balcony window, looking out over the horizon, and when I am outdoors and see a pair of birds, which I do quite often lately, I always think of my mother and father.

Currently, I view death quite differently than I once did. Why should it bring such sorrow? Why should we make part of someone's life sad or tragic? We are joyous when someone is born, but why are we so unhappy when something occurs that we believe to be inevitable and even natural?

If it were true that after we die it is the end, then it would be incredibly sad, but that is not the case. We are Living Beings, souls having a Human experience. When we pass on, we continue to whatever lies beyond the human adventure. If a person's death is truly the successful conclusion of a contract, which they agreed to prior to being born, then it should be a satisfying event, something like a perfectly completed project.

Well-Being

Well-being is determined by the amount of *life-sustaining* energy in our Light Body. Everything in the universe is made up of energy, each particle of which vibrates at its own frequency. The total combined vibration of the particles that comprise each of us, determines our level of awareness, consciousness, well-being, and happiness.

Negative energy vibrates below a life-sustaining level, creating an environment for un-wellness, whether it is mental, emotional, spiritual, or physical. This is not to say that every aspect of an individual is at the same level, there may be parts of us that lower or raise the overall vibration.

In other words, we can be physically robust, but we may also have a compromised mental or emotional energetic signature. There are an infinite number of constantly changing scenarios.

A common example is when we are stressed. We may eat healthy food and get plenty of exercise, but still not be at a life-sustaining level. What this really means is that we do not have enough Life Force Energy to support a state of well-being, because we are using too much of it to counteract the stress, so we become depleted.

Taking control of our well-being.

If we reduce the amount of stress we are experiencing, our level of Life Force Energy increases, and we feel better. The process is unique for each one of us. That is why it is important to take control of our own well-being.

We raise our vibration by exposing ourselves to higher vibrating energy, which is why we feel better in certain situations or in the presence of particular people.

Balance is the measure of wellness. When we are in a balanced physical, emotional, mental, and spiritual state, we will experience well-being. When we are not, we experience unpleasant feelings or un-wellness.

Even if we are not there now, wellness is possible. When we believe that we are well or capable of being so, we have the essential ingredients for a wholesome and healthy life. After that it is up to us to support that healthy state.

The homeopathic method of treating imbalances is based on the premise that energy travels in waves, each substance having its own wavelength. When similar or like waves meet head on, they cancel or nullify one another. For example, when homeopathically treating an allergy, we ingest a substance made up of the allergen, and the allergy *meets its Waterloo* in the form of itself. This can reduce, or even eliminate, the allergic reaction. The fascinating aspect of this, is that homeopathic remedies have the smallest, most minute amount of the allergic substance possible, and that is all it takes.

In a similar fashion, a doctor might prescribe a drug, which acts in the same manner as a homeopathic substance, cancelling the vibration of the symptoms of the disease. The drawback with synthetic substances or pharmaceuticals is that the drug can affect areas of the body that do not need alteration, thereby creating side-effects. The cells must learn to process synthetic chemical substances, that over time may cause the cells to forget how to function normally, which is why we must continue to take certain drugs forever.

Think wellness...

We are all familiar with the placebo effect or the phenomenon that a benign substance can reverse the un-wellness that we are experiencing, thereby producing the same result as an actual remedy or treatment. This illustrates how strongly our beliefs can affect our physical condition. If the wavelength of our *idea* of the disease can cancel the wavelength of the un-wellness, then homeopathically speaking, they have the same vibration.

We know this to be true in the case of stress. When we are stressed, our immune system becomes weaker and we are more susceptible to illness. Over extended periods of time, stress will cause the body to experience other types of un-wellness and conditions that have become all too commonplace. Long term stress, both emotional and environmental, can manifest over time as a deterioration of the physical state. At this point it is much more difficult to reverse the condition without outside treatment, either from a doctor or alternative energy practitioner.

Energy techniques such as Reiki, meditation, yoga, and a myriad of others can remove blocked energy in the affected areas, allowing the Life Force Energy to flow where it previously could not, resulting in an overall increased vibration. This will produce an enhanced feeling of well-being in the mind and body.

You are what you eat.

We all know that food is extremely important in supporting well-being. Fresh food, especially fruits and raw vegetables, can raise our energy level, because they have a higher vibration than processed food. All food, in its natural state, comes from the Earth, and in some way is infused with sunlight and minerals, whether directly or otherwise.

Unlike plants that can synthesize light directly, we must eat plants, or animals that eat plants, to benefit from the sunshine, minerals, and other nutrients that the plant or animal has absorbed during its life cycle. Our physical bodies then integrate the energy of the food as we digest it. In addition, the gratitude we offer for the food that we eat, raises the vibration even higher. Processed food has the opposite effect, as does feeling guilty about eating.

When we eat fresh, unprocessed, organic food, it connects us to the Earth. Unfortunately, many do not eat natural food, resulting in a disconnect from nature in varying degrees. The evidence of this is clearly visible.

We are told that it is beneficial to our health to eat natural, organic, unprocessed, chemical free food, and that foods that contain additives are unhealthy and may cause un-wellness, but it is not explained exactly why.

Natural and organic foods vibrate at a much higher level than processed food, for the simple reason that when chemicals and pesticides are added to food, it lowers the vibration of the food. When we eat the good, clean stuff, it invigorates us by nourishing us with the energy of the Earth and the Sun.

Health Care?

Health Care is one of the primary concerns of modern-day life, but I am astounded that in a culture that claims to be so advanced, wellness is not as common as it should be.

Modern health care practices focus on treating, not preventing.

Once we eat only the best foods, then we must work on *the big one*, our thoughts and feelings. This is important because our thoughts have their own vibration as well. Non-life sustaining thoughts can weaken us, so imagine the effect on an entire population frequently exposed to commercials and media stories about different disorders and the pharmaceutical treatments for those problems.

Each one of these ads, including the disorder they refer to, has its own vibration. If we were to listen to such messages, week after week, and month after month, not only would they lower our energy level, but we would become very compatible with the vibration of the un-wellness that the advertisements describe.

It is truly a clever marketing strategy for making unwellness and prescription drugs seem normal. Even when we are thinking about these conditions, hoping we do not develop them, we are still focusing our thoughts on what we do not want.

There are so many unfortunate things that might happen in a lifetime, that if we place fearful energy on even a fraction of them, we will remain in a negative frame of mind all the time.

Most TV commercials are selling drugs, which is why we are slowly accepting drugs as part of our ordinary reality, as we have breakfast with our family and listen to the morning news.

Commercials are designed to advertise products that we can buy to improve our lives. When we watch a television show, we are in a mildly hypnotic state, making us even more vulnerable to the advertising. We are not completely blocking out the commercial, even though we are not listening. Our mind is paying attention, so we can be aware when the program returns or the next one begins.

We hear other people talk about their drugs and develop a mindset of prescriptions as a part of everyday life. We have plugged into the mass thought form that there is nothing wrong with taking them, because they are approved by the FDA, but that's another story entirely, and the doctor, who certainly knows what he is doing, prescribed them.

You see commercials with people living wonderful lives that they could not have if it were not for the pills they are taking. There is comfort in knowing that whatever happens, there will be a pill, which will allow you to live a normal, healthy life despite your condition. You accept that it is inevitable that you will eventually end up being prescribed a drug, because that is what happens in modern day American life, and you begin to think that it is really not that bad, because everyone is living better lives, as their conditions are controlled and even cured with drugs.

Increasingly, the ads become part of the mass psyche and after a while you even listen to them to see what kind of drugs they are selling. You want to know, because when the time comes you should be informed, forgetting completely that there was a time when people lived healthy lives and never took any prescription drugs. We assume they must have just died when they became ill.

You dare not dream of an existence that might not include medicine, because what if you got sick? What would you do? You could not take a chance on taking herbal supplements or using alternative methods of healing because what if they did not work?

This is the mindset that pharmaceutical companies create, using expensive mainstream advertising. Why are drug commercials and highway billboards for hospitals allowed? The doctor, who went to medical school, is supposed to know what to prescribe, why should we have to ask our doctor? These ads are creating a mass mindset. And you thought you were just getting a weather report?

In the 1939 film, Five Little Peppers and How They Grew, the actor Clarence Kolb plays J.H. King, a wealthy businessman who becomes involved with the Pepper family, a kindly clan that has suffered the death of the father and been thrown into hard times.

Throughout the movie, Mr. King learns the true treasures of family, caring, and generosity. One day while visiting them, the children are diagnosed with measles, and he is quarantined for a week in the Pepper home. While there, he must eat their diet of beans for dinner and flapjacks for breakfast.

For years, his doctor has kept him on a special diet that excludes flapjacks and beans, but when King eats these forbidden dishes, he realizes it is the food he loves. He feels better than ever after a whopping three helpings of hotcakes, and when he returns home, he tells the doctor about his new diet and that he has stopped taking all his pills.

"It's those pills that were making me sick, Doc," he says, as they all have a good laugh.

But there is more ...

Healthy food is only part of the wellness picture. We must also keep our energetic signature at a life-sustaining level. The path to well-being includes a continuous effort to increase our awareness and Light Quotient, so that we can vibrate higher. As we stay above a certain energetic level, un-wellness cannot exist.

In the future, our ideas of wellness may be based on calibrating our energetic levels, but in the meantime, we must accept the responsibility of our well-being and place it into our own hands.

Healing comes from within each of us. No person can heal another. In addition, sometimes a Life Contract includes illness or even untimely death. It is not known why we have, on various levels, agreed to some experiences, and how they will affect others in our lives.

Healing is not always curing...

We must do what we feel is right for us and expect the best outcome, keeping in mind that healing is not always curing. It is possible to heal on a spiritual or emotional level, even though the body may not.

All forms of healing have their place. I am not here to speak ill of conventional medicine, no pun intended. What I am saying is that we live in an artificial environment, which contributes to conditions that people living in natural surroundings might never experience. If we find that our physical condition will benefit from a prescription from the doctor, we can be thankful for the opportunity to have care and treatment. It is important to do what is necessary to support our optimal state of well-being.

Ancient Healing

Thanks to modern technology, evidence is surfacing that human civilizations existed on Earth tens of thousands of years ago and longer. Mainstream science is slow to recognize, and even slower to accept, these new findings, but more each day, the evidence cannot be denied.

Those of us who are willing to embrace our ancient forefathers, are learning that they had advanced methods of healing, which used Sacred Geometry in the form of pyramids, along with electromagnetic Ley Lines of the Earth, underground water, and other natural properties of our planet, solar, and stellar systems.

They stored information in crystals, to intensify these natural energy sources, resulting in the amplification of healing spots on the planet. Inhabitants of the Earth in those times knew the locations of these powerful energies and how to use them to balance and restore well-being.

Even today, the residual, innate knowledge of the ability of the Earth to heal us is still known. We go to oceans and lakes for vacations and to relax, because water purifies and cleanses. There is more oxygen by the seashore as the waves break, and bathing in the saltwater draws toxins from our bodies. We travel to power spots and energy vortexes to rejuvenate, and to experience the higher concentrations of Light.

Water has consciousness and memory. As it transforms from its frozen state, due to planetary warming, it returns to the sea, bringing ancient memories of a primordial energy with it.

Is the wisdom of the ancients becoming ours once more? Has the consciousness that once existed on Earth been set free, to be a blessing to those who wished for it and dedicated their lives to manifest it? It is as though a library of consciousness, stored away in ice until the time was right, is returning.

Water is the expression of the Earth's Love, the most essential part of our Third dimensional environment. The water that is melting from the ice, is the purest on Earth today. It never heard of pollution, and never felt the lower vibrations of humanity.

A healing is taking place as all the little molecules of Love that are in that pristine water, and in the anti-matter that surrounds each microscopic particle, are returning to what they left behind when they chose an altered state from liquid to solid. We are here just at the right time to receive the blessing.

The Weight of the World

How did weight become one of the major concerns in our culture and why is it a struggle for so many? Overeating is how we gain weight, but not necessarily the root cause. Overweight, as we call it, is primarily the by-product of a need for emotional protection, ignorance of proper diet, or substance abuse, the substance being food.

In some cultures, the word fat has positive connotations, so it is not an absolute reality that it implies something negative. If someone said to you, *I do not like you, now do what I want*, what do you think would happen? Would you be willing to do what they asked? I think not. The same goes when we tell that to our bodies.

We can temporarily starve ourselves and lose weight, but we will gain it all back, unless we change the eating habits that caused us to gain the weight. We can try several ways of losing weight, each attempt becoming more difficult because of previous failures. At that point we begin to lose confidence, and to dislike our body increasingly with each unsuccessful attempt at weight loss.

It is not the body of the person struggling with their weight that is fat, it is their mind. If we try to fashion an appearance that fits into an ideal created by society, instead of just being ourselves, we will never really succeed even if we lose the weight.

And who says that we need to lose weight anyway? We believe that excess weight makes us unhealthy, but the negative feelings we have towards our body can also contribute to unwellness. We have the power to change the way we think of ourselves. Even if we are at our desired weight, we must also have a positive self-image.

Thinness is the current cultural preference, and an obsession in our society, not an ideal based on absolute truth. We have all seen paintings and sculptures from other periods in history, which portray subjects as well-rounded and robust.

One day, when I was living in the Caribbean, I stopped to greet a male friend of mine sitting on his verandah, looking at a lingerie catalogue that a tourist had left behind.

"I see you are enjoying yourself," I said to him, assuming he was admiring the scantily clad models.

"What's wrong with these women," he replied, "they look sick?"

"Those are highly paid models from the States," I explained.

"They look *maga*," he continued, using the local word for too skinny.

"That is how women like to look in the US."

"Not here, we like a woman with meat on her bones."

There exists today on Earth, a subconscious plot to keep women weak and malnourished, physically, emotionally, and spiritually. Our culture has allowed women to have more power and equality, but it is actually a trick because at the same time they are convinced that this power is achieved by being physically thin, underfed, walking in heels that are damaging to the body, and even undergoing unnecessary surgical procedures in order to feel beautiful. There is nothing attractive about a person who is malnourished, depriving their brain of the nutrients it needs.

Another day back on the island, I was about to walk into a restaurant. Just then an American woman, a tourist, was leaving. She was, shall we say, quite robust. A Belizean woman of comparable size stood behind me, and we both moved out of the doorway to let the woman pass. I greeted the tourist, who said hello to both of us.

As she passed, the local woman said to her, *Hey, fat girl*. I held my breath, waiting to see what was going to happen. The American woman appeared momentarily horrified, until the Belizean woman finished the sentence with, *you're fat like me!*

In a split second, the American had experienced one of the best parts of her vacation. She came to the Caribbean to see the local culture and she was getting a first-hand experience that was not in any guidebook. Her look of horror melted into a smile of sisterly camaraderie with the local woman, who returned her happy expression and gave her a high five. It was an event which allowed the tourist to transcend the negative images she had about her weight and be part of a truly magical moment with a woman who was comfortable in her own skin.

I have always been careful to not blindly follow trends and mainstream current thought forms of my culture. When I see everyone doing something, I am cautious about *following in their footsteps* until I decide if it is right for me.

Many concepts, which we believe to be true, are ideas that are not only false, but also harmful to our well-being. One such area that has overwhelmingly consumed most of the population, is *weight*. No pun intended…

Weight loss is a billion-dollar industry. Now, let us stop and think about this. No one who is making money from weight loss products really wants us to lose weight, or else how will they keep making money.

Be comfortable in your own skin.

Let us back up a little and define what exactly we mean by overweight. Our culture has created an ideal, having to do with body size. Now, we all know that everyone is physically different, some tall, others short, and the rest in between, but we are encouraged to weigh a certain amount based primarily on our height. Therefore, we can safely assume that expecting everyone to be the same size and weight, according to the current cultural preference, is an unattainable goal, and does not even make sense.

Focusing on weight and the unwarranted negative self-image associated with certain body types, is focusing on what we do not wish to keep around.

For those who are thin by nature, being thin is a healthy physical state, but for the rest of us, losing too much weight is usually not in our best physical interest. To reduce body mass to a size that is not compatible with our bone structure, but is with a young woman on the cover of a magazine that has most likely been photo edited anyway, we must eat less food than our body requires.

In addition, the type of food that has become associated with weight loss is often laden with chemicals and has little fat. The brain needs a certain amount of fat to function properly.

We use the word *food* very loosely. Chemicals are not foodstuff, and processed foods have lost most of their nutritional value. Our bodies are not designed to digest synthetic substances.

Artificial sweeteners are not food, they are chemicals that distress the alkaline/acid pH balance of the body and can cause serious health issues and even addiction. They also create carbohydrate cravings, leading to weight gain.

The current methods of farming food, environmental pollution, soil depletion due to single crop farming practices, fertilization, and genetically modified seeds, have robbed our food of many nutrients, causing us to crave the foods that have these vitamins and minerals. One solution is to take nutritional supplements, but this varies from person to person.

As a culture, instead of seeing others as perfectly where they are supposed to be, we focus so much on thinness that we divide people into two categories, those who are thin and those who are not.

When we are not hungry anymore…it is time to stop eating.

As I sat in front of a food court, filled with throngs of people consuming mostly junk food, I began to think about the situation at hand. It was dinnertime and after a long afternoon of walking in the mall and shopping, many people had worked up an appetite or just felt like eating. I walked amongst the tables topped with burgers, pizza, and fries, noticing that there were excessive amounts of food in front of most people, even children.

Our bodies let us know how much food we require. In other words, when our cells call for nourishment, we get truly hungry. If we eat slowly, chewing and swallowing our food with care, we will know when we have had enough, because we will not feel hungry anymore. The old adage of *clean your plate* is fine if there is not too much food on the plate to start with, but I have a sneaking suspicion that when that saying came into being, there was not the amount of food readily available as there is now. Food had to be prepared. People did not just reach into the refrigerator or go out to a restaurant any time they felt like it.

Social pressure to be thin, and the implications of being overweight, a term applied to a measurement that exceeds a number arrived at by the medical community and/or the fashion industry, has the result of creating low self-esteem. Beauty is big business. There is a disproportionate amount of focus place on whether a person is beautiful. In fact, the person can be amongst the worst scoundrels ever to live and if he or she is beautiful, they hold our attention and earn our admiration. Inner beauty is highly under-valued and outer attractiveness, even though it can be bought, is the measure of a person.

Memo: You do not need to keep weighing yourself. First of all, you must know when you have gained or lost weight if you are aware of your body and if nothing else, your clothes will feel tighter or looser. Secondly, if you have not lost your desired weight, you will get frustrated and eat more. Remember, your weight is not a measure of your self-worth, it is a measure of the mass of your body. You are not better if you weigh less, you only weigh less.

Fall in Love with YOU!

When it comes to shopping, stores keep larger people separate, so that thinner ones do not have to shop with them, as anyone who wears plus size clothing will tell you. The plus size departments hide in basements and corners of stores in areas where no one goes. Often, the clothes are not stylish and usually they cost more, as if an extra two inches of fabric between a size 16 and 1X is going to make a difference in the cost of creating the garment. Why can't these items be amongst the regular clothes? Are we to hide people away who are an inch larger than the privileged, acceptable thin ones?

If we begin loving ourselves the way we are right now, our bodies will respond. We are going to spend our current lifetime in our body, so there is no point in going through our days disliking our appearance. We loved our body when we were born, there is no reason not to love it NOW.

When we think of someone we love, whether romantically, a friend, or a family member, and recall how we feel when we think of them, we can capture that feeling and apply it to the way we think of ourselves.

Our Higher Selves love us no matter what. It is that part of us that was born loving us, and always will.

That part of us does not care how much we weigh, the color of our hair, or how many wrinkles we have. It is eternal, existing in conjunction with our body during this lifetime.

Be the vibrant person that you were born to be.

A young child that loves an adult, does not judge the way that person looks, they just love them. In the same way, our Higher Self loves us unconditionally. We can tap into that feeling and apply it to ourselves any time we feel like it. The standards that society has set for beauty, which are fleeting, keep us from feeling Self-Love. We are each a beautiful creation of the Universe. When our mothers and fathers first saw us, they could not imagine anyone more beautiful, so when we believe that we are healthy and lovely, it is the reality we will endeavor to create in our lives.

Out With the Old

The first rule of Feng Shui is to get rid of clutter in our home and all other areas of our life. The same way we clean out the basement or closets, we must eliminate old habits, thoughts, and beliefs that prevent energy from flowing freely. When we clear out the garbage, we can experience an increased sense of happiness and well-being.

Allowing outdated aspects of ourselves to dissolve and fade away, and replacing them with new thought forms such as peace, love, tranquility, kindness, and joy, is an ongoing process. The best way to do this is by paying attention, becoming more conscious of what we are thinking, and taking the time to evaluate and determine if our thoughts and habits are still valid for our best interest.

If we are struggling to achieve a goal and we encounter resistance, perhaps it is time to focus, not only on that one goal but on the best outcome. This allows for an even better result than the one we envisioned.

A few years back, I decided I wanted a job working with databases, but something always seemed to happen just as I was about to get a job in that field. One day it occurred to me that this might not be my path in life, so I changed my focus to what I really wanted, which was a career in writing.

Soon afterwards, I got an assignment at work writing a technical manual. At the same time, I began to publish my books. When the clutter is gone, the energy will flow. Oddly enough, when I stopped trying to get the database job, another technical job came my way, which included working with databases.

How to Waste Time

Worrying is a waste of time and energy. If we worry about something and it works out, we worried for nothing and we have only made the situation worse by placing our focus on a result we do not want, thereby helping to enable it.

When we allow events to unfold naturally, envisioning the best outcome, we are using our energy and thoughts to create the desired results. Allowing ourselves to believe that things will turn out well and that the universe will supply solutions, is the magic of life.

When I moved to New Jersey from Canada in 2000, it was exceedingly difficult to find an apartment, but I *knew* I would find a suitable place to rent. One day, a friend of mine, who did not share my faithful attitude, said to me, "You're never going to find a good place in your price range. It's impossible."

"Would you just try and be a little more positive," was my reply. The next day, out of frustration, I opened the phone book, *yes*, the phone book, and looked up apartments in the yellow pages. I called the first management company in the list and asked if they had any vacancies. They said they had a one-bedroom unit that I could see any time. I drove there on my lunch hour to have a look and as I pulled up the shady, tree-lined street where the garden apartment complex lay nestled, I was sure this would be my new home.

The manager showed me the freshly painted apartment with newly refinished wood floors and three large windows in the living room, overlooking a courtyard filled with trees. It was perfect. I said I would take it, but the manager explained that another woman had just seen the place and she also wanted it. I asked if I should fill out an application anyway, and he said," Sure, why not?"

I only had a glimmer of hope to get the apartment, but it seems that is all it took. At eleven o'clock the next morning I got a call from the management company, saying that the other person had not faxed her application and they were inquiring if I still wanted the apartment. I told them I did and that I would be there in an hour with the money. It was Friday and I had just deposited the paycheck for the first week of my new job, but I knew it would not clear until Monday.

The management company assured me they would not deposit my check until Monday, so I signed the rental agreement, got the key, went up to my new home, lay down on the newly refinished bare floor, and breathed a sigh of triumph. I was so elated I did not even care that I only had twenty dollars left to my name and a temporary job. I knew it would all work out and you know what, it did.

Life is a dance, learn to move with the rhythm.

How do we stop worrying? First, we must have the intention to do so, and then realize we are in control of our thoughts. We do not have to worry about anything. Worrying is a habit we learned. We did not worry as children. Life is not supposed to be full of things going wrong.

Consider nature, everything is perfect in the natural world and we are part of that world, so why should we experience mishap after mishap. When we go with the flow, and watch life unfold perfectly, we see it the way it is meant to be.

Regret is another waste of time. If we regret something, we are still putting our energy and thoughts into what we wish had occurred differently. If we continue to regret, we will also end up regretting all the time we spent regretting. A better approach is to realize that everything that happened was necessary to get us to where we are now, so it was all good.

Suffering is giving away our power to become a victim. It is the product of a mentality of scarcity. We live in a universe of infinite abundance, why should there be lack? We are not here to suffer. We are not here to suffer. We are not here to suffer. We are here to be happy and enjoy life.

Many people are truly suffering. There are others who choose to unnecessarily suffer along with them. We cannot solve issues from within the system that created them. We cannot rid the Earth of poverty in a culture that allows greed, and we cannot cure illness if we do not recognize wellness as our natural state. Some of us believe that suffering as an inevitable part of life and choose to suffer, rather than not.

A more valuable approach is to continue to hold the Light, so that those that are suffering can see that there still is a Light.

Recent World Events

Many of us wonder why tragedies such as earthquakes, hurricanes, and wars occur. We know that the Earth is evolving, the Ascension process is accelerating, and many believe that everything happens as it should, according to Divine Plan.

But even though such events are tragic, sometimes the best of human nature makes an appearance at such times. The amount of Love, Light, prayers, healing energy, and good wishes magnifies exponentially for those that are suffering.

People become generous with their time and resources. We often witness numerous acts of courage and kindness, even towards total strangers. Real heroes emerge.

In the wake of horror and disaster for some, those not directly affected, create powerful waves of healing energy. Those of us who are bringing in energy from the higher realms, create a level of awareness that the Earth has not seen for ages. During times of destruction and despair, like a beautiful flower growing out of the cracks in the sidewalk, humankind is being inspired to generate enormous amounts of Love.

The Re-emergence of Reiki

Under such circumstances, Reiki resurfaced in Japan in 1945. When I say it re-surfaced, there is evidence that it existed in ancient times, but as a blessing, it was re-discovered, in good and perfect time. Many of us began our journey of Conscious Human Evolution, learning Reiki. It is a powerful tool.

I am a MerKiVa Reiki Master, a system of Reiki which I developed, which combines Sacred Geometry with traditional Reiki symbols. I still give myself some Reiki nearly every day, while falling asleep or even driving.

We are here to hold the Light.

As a result of tragic events, in which there is suffering for many, we often re-evaluate belief systems, allowing us to make great strides in clearing negative, lower vibrating energy.

When we experience unsettling world events, whether first-hand or not, we are provided with a real-life exercise in holding the Light from the higher dimensions and remaining observers of what is happening. Those of us who are Masters recognize that part of our purpose for being here is to maintain our vibration at the highest level possible, so that when these events occur, and the Light is needed the most, we are able to provide it.

As always, the more Love, Light, and Healing Energy we can create, the more we are contributing to the best possible outcome for humanity and the Earth. As we continue to do this, it becomes as much a part of us as breathing. As we hold the Light, we are opening the pathways for others to also increase their Light quotient.

The New Era is here. It is complete and functional. Those of us who place our focus on the higher dimensions, are the Light-Bringers of the new Crystalline energy, into which we are all evolving. We are in our appointed spot on the Earth's Dodecahedral grid, holding it in place and keeping it intact. There is no going back now, no failure or questions as to whether the Ascension Process will occur, because it already has.

We are an instrumental part of the process, as we continue on our paths. When we do not know what to do next, we can always ask our Angels and guides to help us. If we are unsure of the next step, we must only wait for an answer, and it will not be long. We are the Bright Stars of the present and the future. We are the driving force of the Divine Ray of Hope for all. We must shine our Love Light for all to see, and walk into the unknown with excitement and wonder.

Only the Good Stuff

Only the good stuff! That is what I invoke before I eat my food, but it also applies to other aspects of life. Each day, we find ourselves bombarded by negative thoughts and information, designed to lower our energy level, and transform us into consumers of products that can help us raise it back up. It sounds ridiculous when we think about it, but we should not take it lightly at all.

By using discretion, we determine the energy we allow into our Light Body, avoiding what takes away our power, lowers our energy level, or makes us energetically weaker.

When we do not resonate with a particular energy, whether it is a person, food, situation, or any part of our life, we sense it in our gut. Most of us have had such feelings, if we are paying attention. As soon as we align ourselves with the energy we *do* resonate with, we feel better. When we think happy thoughts, our body knows. Imagine the effect that a steady stream of violent media has on our energy body, if one negative thought can weaken us.

By filtering the information coming into our consciousness, it is possible to remain happy and peaceful, even when things around us seem otherwise. When we are transparent, being in the world and deciding in what way we will take part, we can hold more Light, and send it back out into the world.

It is not nobler to be part of the demise of civilization, or to tune into aspects of our culture that are not life-sustaining, and it most certainly does not help those who choose to participate in the lower levels of consciousness.

Life is a process of unfolding.

Humankind is currently changing so rapidly that no one can afford to waste time on negativity. As an example of how fast our civilization is evolving, we can consider the rate at which technology advances. We are changing faster than that, since we are creating it. Every day some new technological discovery appears. It is nonstop, especially considering that when we are sleeping, others are working, and making discoveries. When we awaken, the world has changed.

These advancements are not the product of negative thoughts. Instead, they are born from hopeful visions of those who only see possibilities. The wave of the present and the future is based on looking at the bright side, the positive aspects, and desires of our heart.

Living this way, requires some adjustments. We must check our thoughts and what we allow to influence us. In addition, we do not have to listen to anyone else's negativity. We can change the subject or just not pay attention. Many people like to dump negative energy on others, but we must not be one of the *dumpees*. This may mean ending relationships with friends or loved ones. If this happens, then we can accept that the person is not meant to be part of our life at this time.

It is our responsibility to filter what we allow into our Light Bodies. It is a matter of self-preservation. It is all part of the process of Conscious Human Evolution.

Part II

Evolving Into the Higher Realms

I Stepped Off a Cliff and Didn't Fall

When I was younger, I never really knew what I wanted. However, I knew what I did not want. I stood on the Cliff of Conformity and saw only one way to go, and that way was to step off into the unknown.

Most of my life, what I saw around me seemed so dull and drone. There had to be something else, I knew there must be. I heard about love and romance from the little 45 rpm records I played over and over, and I experienced passion, adventure, excitement, and magic in the movies I saw and the books I read. I wanted those things in my life, and I knew that behind me on the cliff was BORING!

I had no fear as I stepped off, for I knew somehow that I was protected. The best part was I was right. I began to follow my own path and do things my own way. Sometimes it was painful, difficult, and lonely, other times it was exciting and fun. What kept me going was the certainty that I did not want to be like everyone else, following the crowd.

After a while, things became easier, and I began to see that there was no need for struggle. I perceived myself as an amazing person who took the chance to follow my own guidance, and I survived. I began to be proud of myself for my courage, and I wanted to share with others what I had learned so they could live a happy, pleasant life too. So, I began to write it all down so that those who read my books might find the encouragement to follow their own path as well. That is what I wish for everyone.

Oh, the cleverness of me! - Peter Pan

We are all amazing, if we will only recognize it. Staying connected to feelings and intuition, guides us into the unknown as we rise to our higher potential and integrate the many innovative changes and shifts that are happening.

Each of us is involved in the Ascension Process, either consciously or unconsciously; however, when we become aware of our higher purpose, we can take part in it, more gracefully and seamlessly.

Holding more Light, makes us more Enlightened.

The process of en-Lightening is simple. If we recall an unpleasant memory of an earlier event, and we again feel, the emotions we felt then, we can change what happened by releasing those emotions, and filling the space they once occupied with Light.

Everything that happens is either to *teach* us or *serve* us, there are no mistakes. We all do the best we can with what we have to work with at the time. If we think that someone else can do better, it is only because we have already learned what they have not. Therefore, what happened in the past was the best we could have done at the time. Hopefully, we will not find ourselves in a similar situation again, now that lessons have been learned.

Really Happy

If we wish to participate in the Ascension Process, we must first be happy. Happiness is highly underrated as a simple emotion, but it is much more than that. The amount of Light we are receiving, integrating, and sending, is the measure of how happy we are. Therefore, it is to our advantage to let go of anything that is interfering with us being happy.

Life is full of amazing and fascinating events and people. When we consciously take part in shining our Light, so that others will know there IS a Light, we are taking part in one of the greatest events that we have yet to experience. The New Era is dawning, and we are a part of it, embracing it in Love and Light.

Really Real

Just being positive is not enough though. Our beliefs must also evolve. What is true for us today, might only be a steppingstone to a higher reality tomorrow. Truth is only true right now, and what is true for one person may not be true for another. We are the only ones who know what is true or right for us, and the way we know is through our feelings and intuition.

There are two kinds of feelings: emotions, fed by our ego, and *knowing*, which has its source in our connection with our Higher Self. *Knowing* is what we truly believe at a soul level.

Others may think they know what is right for us, but they only have knowledge of what is right and true for them. When we receive advice, intended to be for our benefit, we can use our *feelings* to determine if we resonate with the suggestions.

Even if we are not certain about what is in our best interest, happily our Higher Self does. The Higher Self is the part of us that connects us to the Source of everything. We must become aware of our connection to that higher part of ourselves, to receive the guidance.

Gradually, we can let go of the conditioning that we learned as children and create our own beliefs. The old ways are dying, and new concepts are being born. We can reach for the stars, for it is where we originated.

Really Calm

As we ascend, we learn to remain calm and heart centered. In many situations this can be challenging, but with practice we can learn to return to our Heart Center any time we wish, focusing our awareness from the brain, which is processing the environment around us, to the center of our being.

From the Heart..

When we begin to think with our heart, we tend to forget our cares and stress. There are many effective tools that can help us in this process. The Violet Flame of Transmutation is profoundly effective in clearing negative energy from our Light Body.

Wherever we might be, we can invoke the Violet Flame, visualizing it blazing up from under our feet and surrounding us with a cool Violet translucent light that transforms the particles of negative energy into clear, positive, life-sustaining ones.

When I become aware of a negative thought, I stop, focus on my Heart Center, remain focused in the moment, and call in the Violet Flame. Soon I feel the cool, soothing purple energy clearing the lower vibrations.

We can visualize the Violet Flame under our bed when we go to sleep, or beneath us when we meditate.

I invoke the Violet flame when clearing crystals, and I stand in it when I take my gemstone jewelry off at night to cleanse the stones. When we sit down to eat, the Violet flame can clear our food. There are many creative ways to take advantage of this blessing and gift from the Ascended Master Saint Germain.

Getting stoned...

Crystals are sentient beings waiting to work with us. They can help modify the energetic integrity of our Light Body. As we take part in the Process of Conscious Human Evolution, our cells become more compatible with a Crystalline structure, making it extremely beneficial to allow crystals, to assist us in the process.

Wearing crystal jewelry is an effective way to have stones near us during the day. If we are unsure which stone to work with, there are many books and lots of information online, but I always find that trusting my feelings about being drawn to a stone is the best way to know that that stone wishes to work with me.

An Alpha State – the place to be...

Listening to calm, soothing music is another way to remain centered. One of the most sublime pieces of music ever written is Dvorak's Symphony No. 9 "From the New World". Hearing it brings me to a place of serenity.

Reading inspiring books or doing a reading on inspirational cards before going to sleep, can make a difference in our quality of rest. By doing so, we align our energy level with the inspired messages we read. I download digital card decks on my phone, so I can get inspired any time I like.

Trusting Ourselves

As we learn to trust that we can make wise decisions that improve our lives, we can let go of feeling it is necessary to do what everyone else does, and then blame society when things do not turn out the way we expect.

Even when our choices are unique, we can trust that our decisions are right for us. If we are doing something or going somewhere because we think we *should*, but it is not really what we want to do, we can re-evaluate the situation to see if we still wish to proceed in that direction, make new plans, or just relax. Doing nothing, is really doing a lot.

How would we feel if someone said that he or she did not trust us? That is the same way we will feel, in our center or Solar Plexus, when we do not have confidence in ourselves. Messages are coming to us all the time, we only must look and listen for them, acknowledge them when they arrive, and recognize the blessing of guidance coming through from the

Higher Realms. In doing so, we attract people who also believe in themselves and in us.

As I reflect on the events that have occurred in my life, I do not understand every one of them as some have been quite strange, but I know they were all part of a voyage that brought me to where I am today, and I would not change any part of it. In the rational, logical Third Dimension, my journey made little sense. In fact, it is the tale of a woman who had no purpose, goals, or any of the usual pursuits that most women have. But at the level at which I was vibrating at the time, it was perfect.

We are all energetic beings with unique vibrations, our own Soul Song, so to speak. I will not go into a lengthy scientific or metaphysical discussion, which would fill chapters on the quantum structure and atomic makeup of our existence, for I do not necessarily accept as absolute truth the explanations that science offers us.

It is not that I disbelieve what has been scientifically proven, but the limitations of the technology that scientists have at their disposal, tends to render results that are only part of the picture.

Neither will I offer you the theories and beliefs of New Age knowledge, which I cannot scientifically prove. By the way, the only real difference between scientific and New Age thought is that science must prove, using their own deductive methods, that which spiritual seekers already know.

We, the evolutionary pioneers, have the advantage of being able to use our feelings to validate truth and beliefs. This frees us to move on to the next step, the next level, and the next big discovery. Our method of validation uses a reliable source of guidance, obtained by trusting ourselves and moving fearlessly into the new frontiers of life, in the pursuit of Conscious Human Evolution.

In the magical realm of the 1960's, when new belief systems were being born, it was common to hear it said that a person had *a good or bad vibe*. The wisdom inherent in the recognition that people, places, and situations have their own vibration, was an innocent view of what Quantum physicists are postulating and proving. All life is drawn to the vibrations it resonates with. It is our means of survival.

I find myself in a very uncommon circumstance, having lived on the fringes of society for most of my adult years. At times I wondered why my life was so unusual. When I was seven years old, I was convinced that my life was only a dream, and that I would awaken into my real one. I envisioned a group of beings in a control-center type structure, watching everything we do. I did not know then that I was consciously aware of the Cosmic Council of Light, the group of Ascended Masters, Archangels, and Light Beings who watch over us.

I passionately hoped to fly away in a UFO to another planet, which is interesting, since we all have interplanetary heritage from Sirius, Pleiades, Orion, and other star systems. The upside of spending my life on the outside of my culture is that it made it easier for me to change my ideas and beliefs.

There currently exists a growing number of us, who realize that their purpose on Earth is to contribute to the transformation, transmutation, and evolution of the planet and its inhabitants. We are the ones who are paving the way for humanity to move into the Higher Realms. But we should remember that indigenous peoples have held the Light for ages, so that we did not sink into total darkness, with no hope of ever ascending higher.

Many of us are consciously part of the Ascension process, facilitating this major evolutionary quantum leap, by taking part as conduits for increased Light and Life Force Energy, more than the inhabitants of Earth have seen for an exceptionally long time. It is what we have chosen to do, it is our destiny, and it is what matters to us. Our male and female energies are becoming balanced, and we will again become the Luminous Light Beings we once were.

I had wonderful, loving parents. I believe I chose them because they allowed me to nurture my own identity as I grew up under their care. They did not force their beliefs on me, which allowed me the freedom to form my own ideas, and I was able to make choices that I might not have made otherwise.

I stayed in my own wonderful world, in which music was my savior. I listened to 45 rpm Rock n' Roll records on a little record player that allowed me to stack a dozen or so on the spindle or play one over and over. A great new song transported me to another world, one filled with the hope of true love.

My goal became finding the person with whom I would share the level of emotion expressed in the lyrics of the songs I heard, the romantic movies I watched, and the books I read. What I did not understand was that not everyone else felt the same way.

In addition, the level of integrity of the society in which I was living was steadily declining. Little by little the moral structure of my country, and the world in general, was thinning like an old piece of fabric. Of course, if you read literature from centuries past, the same claims are made about society then, but we are only witness to the changes of our own times.

*Give me music that moves me,
the kind that makes me go.*

Love was not the only message pouring out of the songs of the 50's, the emergence of the wildness that had been repressed in humans for so many thousands of years was the driving force of *Rock n' Roll*. Like a bear awakening from hibernation, the primordial energy that had been asleep for ages was releasing, and there was no going back. We were dancing again, wildly, with abandon, passion, drive, joy, and FUN!

Some of our elders were outraged, they could not resonate with the Rock music, it was more than they could tolerate, but there was nothing they could do about it, for we could not be stopped. All we wanted to do was to hear the songs that excited us. It was beyond sensuality. It was true earth-bound wildness generated from the lower chakras.

The reason Elvis swiveled his hips was not only to entice, but it was where the music moved him. In similar fashion, many indigenous dancers also move from the waist down, keeping their upper bodies relatively motionless.

The music of the 50's was awakening the root and sacral chakras of teenagers who were lucky enough to be at the right age at that time. I was too young to have male dance partners in the 50's, and when my family moved to a new town in the early 60's, my upscale classmates were not much interested in that era of rock and roll. Instead, something new, of which until then I had been unaware, had been born.

Too late to stop now!

The Age of Aquarius, the generation of love, freedom, hippies, and the beginning of the end of the old ways had begun. No one told me, but the kids in the new town where my family moved when I was sixteen, were *hipper* than me and they knew all about it.

On summer nights we went to Greenwich Village in New York City, a quick twenty-minute drive, in my old '51 Plymouth. We strolled amongst the throngs of people that gathered on MacDougal Street and went into little basement clubs to hear the new *underground music*.

By the time I went away to college, things had changed, and new choices were before me. Men had longer hair and women looked more natural. I knew right away it was time to leave the old behind and step into the new. My principal motivation in life is avoiding boredom, which always keeps me searching for the latest. That is why Conscious Human Evolution is now my primary focus, the purpose, and most enjoyable part of my life.

Be Here Now

Awareness is the degree to which we are present. What we are aware of is consciousness, the raw material of existence. As we go through our days, thinking ahead of all we must do, and rushing about to get here and there, unless we are focused on what is happening right now, we are missing much of our lives.

Suppose we knew there was only one more day to spend here on Earth, we would savor every moment, appreciating what we normally take for granted, and realizing the preciousness of our life and those in it.

The time to begin to put things in their proper perspective is now, right now, not tomorrow and not even ten minutes from now, for each moment is an opportunity and a gift. As we go through our everyday activities, there is much more going on than appears.

We have the opportunity to connect with people we encounter in shops, and we can smile at others that pass our way. We are interacting with these people for a reason. We may have known them in another lifetime or be connected to them in a different dimension. They might even be Angels, taking a human form to interact with us. Our actions here might affect what is happening elsewhere.

When we prepare our food, we can be grateful for the animals and plants that gave their lives for our dinner. How often do we consider them and the existence they lived, so that we may have ours? If we were that chicken or cucumber, on some level they had consciousness, and on another plane, they valued that life, expressed by the fact that they survived. The offer of thanks from the person who was benefitting from their existence, might be meaningful. Do we even think of what it would be like to live to be consumed by another?

It does not take long to appreciate what we have and express gratitude. Each day has many opportunities for us to be aware of what else is going on besides us and our needs. This is what having awareness means and as we develop this ability, we will be amazed at the amount of activity that is occurring and that we have been missing.

We can begin by observing our immediate surroundings in new and different ways. Listening to the birds sing and the wind blow through the trees, allows us to hear them talking to us and sending us messages. When the breeze begins to blow at a significant moment, or when we see birds on the telephone wires, spiritual energy is being transmitted. These are things to take note of, because it means a message is coming our way. Subtle activity is occurring all day long, in our immediate surroundings. All we must do is to notice…

Believe It

There are many mass thought forms that we believe to be absolutely true. However, at other times in history there existed different ideologies that were just as valid to those who believed them, as ours are to us. With that said, I will now try to rock the boat of the current belief systems of our culture and expose those who are holding us back with invisible shackles.

In the movie Lost Horizon, directed by Frank Capra, and one of my favorite movies of all time, Robert Conway, a British diplomat, is escaping war-torn China in the 1930's. His plane, carrying a few others, is hijacked, and is taken to a remote place in the Himalayas, which turns out to be the paradise called Shangri La.

Over time Conway wants to stay, but other members of his party convince him that he is not meant to be there and that they all should leave. During the arduous journey through the snow-covered mountains, he realizes that he was wrong to leave

Shangri La. The two others in his party die in a fall. He trudges on, not knowing in which direction he is going. Finally, he arrives at a small village, when the local inhabitants find him unconscious.

After he recovers, the authorities attempt to return him back home to England, but he escapes and by any means possible, stealing, fighting those who try to restrain him, and accomplishing superhuman feats of traversing the treacherous Himalayan Mountains alone, he risks everything to return to the paradise he abandoned.

A colleague, who had set out to find him, returns to London with only the legend of Shangri La and Robert Conway, the man who defied the limitations of humanness. As he tells the incredible tale to some of the members of his posh London club, they ask him if he believes the story. He says, *Yes, I believe it, because I choose to believe it.*

We choose to believe.

Choosing to believe in something is what we all do. As incredulous as the reality of Shangri La is for some of us to believe, our truths might be just as fantastic to others, it is all relative.

On Caye Caulker, Belize, my home for fifteen years, many of the men on the island were fisherman.

Occasionally they fished at night during the full moon, when certain types of fish were biting. I was told that care must be taken to cover the fish from the light of the full moon or else the side of the fish, upon which the moonlight shone, would spoil and the meat would get soft very quickly.

We, as a culture, are not especially aware of the energy generated by moonlight. In fact, I would venture to say that most people do not even look up at the moon or keep track of the phases of its cycles, as people in other cultures do.

When I first heard that fish story, I did not believe it, but after asking several experienced fishermen, who confirmed its truth, I changed my mind.

While living on the island I rented snorkeling gear to tourists. One day a couple came in and told me that they had been snorkeling with a local guide who was also spear fishing. They explained that the Mayan diver stayed under the water for *a very long time*. This day they brought their watches with the intention of timing how long the diver remained under the water. When they came back, they told me, in utter amazement, that he was under the water for twelve minutes on one breath. I would not have believed it if they had not timed it, but it is true.

There are plants that grow on Earth that are remedies for practically every ailment known to man, even to animals. There are large numbers of people who live long, healthy lives. I know this to be true because I have seen them. There are jungle bush doctors, using what some may call *magic*, and New Age practitioners using energy techniques that help people heal, even when all other methods fail.

So, you see, even though we believe something is true, it does not necessarily make is so for everyone. Then is there an absolute truth? We like to believe that there is, because it makes us feel secure, by validating our beliefs, but the only belief we need to make us feel secure is knowing that we ARE secure.

Self-Esteem

Now we come to the big one, self-esteem, or the opinion we have of ourselves. Healthy self-esteem is an essential part of the Process of Conscious Human Evolution, including how we treat ourselves and others and being aware that we deserve everything we desire.

I deserve all that I desire, and things always go well for me.

It is easy for self-esteem to be diminished in everyday life, as we are constantly bombarded with unattainable ideals, intended to turn us into perpetual consumers. We are made to feel fearful, unwell, and unhappy, so that we continue to buy things to make us feel better. It seems to be working on a grand scale.

We literally *buy into* the scheme, rather than setting our own standards and feeling good about ourselves for doing so. As a result, we grow up learning to gauge our self-worth by what we own and how we look. By the time we are adults, we characterize ourselves according to our job, car, clothes, house, and a myriad of other toys and possessions. We become so diverted by all these things that we neglect to value or develop our standards and character. The result is a steadily increasing level of consumption of products and substances to compensate for the lack of personal fulfillment we have in our lives.

I am not against materialism. I love *stuff*, but possessions will not make us feel good about ourselves. We must be happy with ourselves first and then we can get all the *stuff* we like.

On Caye Caulker island, we were happy to have an empty glass jar with a good plastic top after consuming all the contents. A small article that I would today discard into the recycle bin, was a valuable item for storing food.

Living in paradise gave me a different outlook towards material possessions, as there was not much to buy on the Caye. At that time, the most expensive hotel was about $40 a night, and a fresh lobster dinner was $20. The lack of opportunities to consume, placed everyone on fairly equal financial ground.

The first five years I lived on the island I owned and ran a breakfast restaurant that served only coffee, tea, and fruit crepes with yogurt and granola, homemade by me. The remaining years, I switched occupations and sold the hand-painted artistic t-shirts that I created. One day a couple came into my shop to see my creations, and the woman asked me where she could throw her banana peel.

"Just throw it out the window", I replied, "I will rake the yard later."

"I can't believe I am throwing something out the window," she said, as she tossed the peel, "it's so much fun, I want to move here!"

The little wooden house right on the beach, was on stilts and very old, but the view of the Caribbean Sea and the reef in the distance, was one of the best on the island. Tall palm trees surrounded the house, providing shade most of the day, and the breeze almost always blew through the windows.

It was a comfortable house, but in great need of repair.

"What a beautiful house," she continued.

As I looked at the walls, with open spaces between the boards, and the floor, parts of which were unsafe to walk upon, I replied in true New Jersey style, "It's a slum!"

She only perceived a romantic view of my dwelling. Granted, I loved the house, despite its state.

It is still there, having withstood hurricanes, and I am happy to know that it is now a cybercafé.

> *We are only as happy and successful*
> *as we want to be.*

My self-esteem found me quite unexpectedly one day on the island. I was dating a pirate, whom I will credit with being able to parallel park a sailboat. As I was expressing to him my opinion on the quantity of rum he regularly consumed, he looked at me and said, "You have a problem."

I walked outside onto the veranda, and as I felt the cool Caribbean breeze, my self-esteem hit me square in the face. I had lost it someplace along the way and the breeze must have blown it in.

I began to think about my personal qualities, including the fact that I was the owner of two successful businesses on the island. I went on to acknowledge that I was an intelligent woman with good friends and a wonderful family. I was *on a roll,* thinking of all my good points, including that I was an attractive, educated person who excelled at whatever I set my mind to accomplish.

I walked back inside and said, "You know what, you're right, I do have a problem, YOU! Get out." Of course, pirates do not just get up and leave, so I walked away from my life there and returned to the States. I returned after a year, when I learned he had married someone else.

Five years later, just about the time that my artistic endeavors became tedium, something quite wonderful happened. One of my closest friends, whom I met on the island, offered me a job in the production office of a major motion picture company. I was off to Toronto to work on a film called Finding Forrester, processing digital continuity photos.

I had two weeks to get ready, having never touched a digital camera or a Mac operating system. I put all my focus into the project, and my self-esteem soared because of my successful accomplishments.

After a year or so, it became increasingly difficult for me to work in Canada, so I moved to New Jersey, where I was born and raised. By that time, my computer skills were much improved, and I found a job in the IT department of a large real estate company. I never doubted that everything in my life would work out for the best and it always has. That was my journey, but there are ways to speed up the process of self-Love.

When we begin to look at all our excellent qualities and accept every aspect of ourselves right now, we become magnets for energies that are associated with self-Love. Focusing on the qualities we like about ourselves; the unnecessary ones will fade away when we do not give them attention. Then we can experience the freedom of not needing anyone's approval, but our own.

Success

If someone else can do something, so can I...

There are those who confidently and effortlessly achieve their goals, while others appear to struggle through life. To begin experiencing success we must believe we deserve it.

Many years ago, a woman told me, *Wendy, you are only as happy and successful as you want to be.* The idea that I was in control of my life, and all I had to do was to change my attitude and my beliefs, startled me. I began to practice thinking positive thoughts. During the day I recited mantras such as, *I deserve all that I desire, If someone else can do something, so can I, I am perfectly where I should be every moment, and I am a divine creation.*

Each time I found myself thinking something negative or doubting myself, I practiced my positive affirmations. After a while I did not have to practice anymore, positive thinking became my reality. I began to see that things really do go well when we expect them to.

As we begin to believe that we will achieve our goals, we set the flow of abundance into motion, receive the guidance we need to continue to do so, and know the steps to take in the process. Furthermore, the momentum we experience when things go well, will encourage us to go further. As we see our efforts materialize into the results we desire, we gain confidence in our ability to create successful outcomes.

We live in a universe of infinite possibilities, one of these being that we deserve to have what we truly desire; that is why we wish for it, because we are supposed to have it.

Success means different things to each of us, but what it has in common for everyone is achieving goals. This does not mean we are only successful if we achieve our final goal. Success is an ongoing process of a series of moments, occurring the way we would like, or better.

When exactly do we become a success, or is each small accomplishment a part of the success we achieve during our visit here on Earth? I find that recognizing, celebrating, and showing gratitude for the small successes in my life, paves the way for more to come.

In the Process of Conscious Human Evolution, we allow ourselves the joy of seeing our goals materialize, and we realize that we deserve our success.

Being Grateful

Once we have acknowledged and given thanks for what we have, we are in the position to receive more, as we express gratitude whenever possible. We can always look for the uplifting aspects of any situation and when we hear those doubtful thoughts trying to creep in, telling us that things probably will not work or it is too good to be true, we can just replace them with positive, confident ones.

Gratitude signifies acceptance. It validates the act of receiving.

There is no point in scolding ourselves for being pessimistic, as old energy surfaces from deep within us. Instead we can just the old energy go and be thankful that thoughts are shifting from our subconscious into our conscious, so that we can transmute them. Why hold on to ideas and beliefs, which no longer serve us? *Better out than in,* I always say. Then we can fill the space with Love and Light.

I once took a Reiki class with a mother of three children. She told a story of how she discovered gratitude. For many years she struggled to pay the rent, buy groceries, and provide the most basic needs for her family. One day, after dinner, she sat at her kitchen table, thinking about how little she had in her life. Feeling discouraged, she looked up and saw the pile of dishes in the sink, and reluctantly stood up to wash them.

Suddenly, she viewed the unwashed plates as a symbol of the meal she had happily shared with her family. A wave of gratitude filled her heart.

She opened the refrigerator to put some things away, noticing that it was full. She had earned some extra money that week and had gone grocery shopping. Again, she felt gratitude that she had enough to feed herself and her family for the next few days, without worrying about how she would do it.

She sat down, took out a piece of paper, and began to make a list of everything in her life for which she could feel grateful. The list was longer than she ever could have imagined, and she realized at that moment that her life was full of blessings. From that day on, she continued to appreciate everything she had, and her life began to increase in abundance. Two years later when she told me the story, she had a successful, prosperous healing practice, and was offering seminars on gratitude.

Give thanks.

Expressing gratitude validates our belief in the abundance of the universe, along with our ability to attract and receive that abundance. We are affirming that all we desire will flow into our lives in good and perfect time.

Gratitude is felt in varying degrees. Imagine you have been walking outside for a long time, on an extremely hot day. You are very thirsty and there is no water available. As you continue to walk, you know that you will not be able to get a drink for quite some time. Finally, when you do not think you can bear it any longer, you arrive at a place where water is for sale. The bottle of cool water is so refreshing, that you enjoy it more than any other drinking experience you can remember.

Now imagine you are sitting at home with a glass of water by your side and you take a sip because you are mildly thirsty. You hardly feel grateful for the sip of water since it was only a slight matter of comfort to you.

Gratitude is not just a passing feeling we experience in hopes we will attract more. When we sincerely express genuine gratitude for what we already have in our lives, we are in a position to continue to manifest our dreams.

When we Love our lives, each step, even if we trip, is one more step towards our goals, hopes, and dreams. All our thoughts and actions are the building blocks of our future, and we determine the quality of the building materials we use.

I love my life, and I am grateful for all of it. When I wake in the morning and remember I am back in my existence, I am filled with joy at the prospect of another day on my journey of Conscious Human Evolution. I have placed my focus on creating a lifestyle that includes doing the things that I love.

I have also learned to enjoy the mundane activities and aspects of life. For example, I prefer to live in clean and tidy surroundings, so there is no reason for me to dislike the activities involved in maintaining the standard of cleanliness I prefer.

During the years I lived on the island, I washed my laundry by hand. I enjoyed the process for several reasons. First, washing clothes outdoors in a warm tropical climate can be very refreshing. In addition, I felt akin to the many women on the planet who wash clothing without the help of a machine.

Laundry gets much cleaner when washed by hand and smells fresher when dried on a line in the sun. If left hanging after the sunlight no longer shines, the moisture in the air is a natural fabric softener. Lastly, it was a good workout.

When we experience true gratitude, we are transforming our lives from the mundane into the divine. We create a standard, defined by our thankfulness, which allows only that which is deserving of our gratitude to be part of our life. Sincere gratitude is being thankful for what we have, not because it is better than what someone else has, but because we appreciate that we have it. To put it simply, *it's just plain...being grateful.*

Receiving in a gracious manner is a difficult lesson for some, but in doing so, not only are we getting something, which is fun, but also, we are allowing someone to give, which, in turn, makes them feel good. When a person offers a compliment, we need not diminish it by qualifying it. Instead of saying, *Oh that old thing*, we can just say, *thank you*.

When we graciously receive, we are validating the belief that we are worthy. Giving and receiving are both empowering actions. When we graciously accept what others give to us, we are building a template for abundance.

If I'm So Enlightened…

If I'm so enlightened, why am I working in a corporate environment? This is a question I have asked myself many times. Should I be a full-time writer, doing my own work? Why am I spending my day working in software development?

I have seriously considered pursuing a full-time writing career, promoting the books and articles that I love to create. I imagined that I would get a presentation together and begin lecturing, so I could quit my job and focus on a career that resonates with my esoteric work, but then I began to look at my path in life a little more closely.

To begin with, and most importantly, I enjoy what I do at my corporate IT job. I love technology. In addition, it affords me a comfortable standard of living. I have been able to buy books and attend the seminars that contribute to my spiritual growth. I have been able support two web sites, where I can publish my articles and promote my writing.

I began to realize that one reason I have my job is so I can do my spiritual work and follow my life's purpose, without the stress of lack of money attached to it.

We are all where we are meant to be.

My job has flexible hours, so I do not have to drive in heavy traffic on the forty-mile drive. Many days I work from home, so there is no commute. I enjoy lovely music and the landscape on a good part of the trip to central New Jersey, so when I arrive, I am relaxed and happy. In addition, many of my best ideas for stories and articles come to me while driving.

During the day I have the opportunity to interact with co-workers and enjoy the experience of working on a team with extremely talented people. I meet enlightened people working in my corporate environment, quite a few of whom have pleasantly surprised me with inspiring conversations. And of course, as I love to make people laugh, I manage to lift their spirits throughout the day.

My desk at work has crystals, photos of power spots, a salt lamp, Reiki symbols, in various hidden places, and mandalas. When people step into my cube, they often comment how good the energy feels. This same energy goes out into the building, raising the vibration.

Working in technology keeps me grounded, balanced, and focused. I see my life as *perfectly perfect* and *moderately moderate,* and my corporate job is part of the plan.

We are all where we are meant to be, and where we can do the most good. As we ascend, in the Process of Conscious Human Evolution, we must remember that the Earth is also undergoing her own changes. This includes the rebuilding of the electromagnetic grid that surrounds the planet, the system of Ley Lines on the surface, and the vortexes that range from the Earth's core to the Higher Dimensions, all of which were once intact, in the distant past.

As we raise our vibration, we are contributing to the reconstruction and restoration of the Earth's energy grid. If we could see a map, depicting where those who are holding the highest energy are geographically located, and how the energy is being used, we would see that we are performing a significantly important task in being where we are. We will know when the time comes for us to move to another location or do something different. In the meantime, we can relish what we do each day, because it matters.

Part III

The Process
of
Conscious Human Evolution

The Garden of Eden

There is a world where life is good, and all is well, and it is right here on Earth. It exists beyond a thin, transparent veil of conscious perception that despite its fragility, has power greater than a thick lead wall for those who live within it.

We are taking part in the Process of Conscious Human Evolution. We live outside *the veil,* appearing quite ordinary at times and at others very unusual. Other may not know that we are different, but we recognize one another through our feelings and vibrations. We live in the everyday world, but ours is a magical land of beauty, synchronicity, pleasant surprises, and friendly folk. We exist on many different economic and social levels, but what we have in common is that in our world, life is good, and all is well.

I am not speaking of a fantasy place on another planet or in a different time, it is right here and right now. We live on a wonderful, rapidly evolving planet, full of fascinating people and places, but we must lift the clouds of illusion that we have grown to accept, and learn to see life as it really is.

In an infinite and abundant universe, inhabited by enlightened, intelligent beings, on a beautiful place such as the Earth, we are not meant to suffer. We have fashioned our world and taken a few wrong turns, but the time has come for us, as luminous life forms, to get back on the journey we came here to experience.

> *Our purpose, is lifting the vibration of others by raising our own.*

Life is amazing and wonderful, but only if we believe it to be so. I not only believe it, I know it. The reason I know it to be true, is because I see it daily. I feel as though I am the luckiest person alive. I exist with the purpose of lifting the vibration of others, by raising my own. I am a *Light-Bringer*, one of many, downloading an increased influx of higher vibrating energies into our world.

Even in the most dismal times in my life, I always believed that everything would work out well, and it did. Today I know everything transpires perfectly, and each part of my life is just the way I would like it. Of course, there is always room for improvement, always another book to write, and continued personal growth, but now it is without struggle.

While people are bemoaning the economy, health issues, relationship problems, and emotional upheaval, I am sailing by in my world of happiness and peace. It might sound selfish to some, but the reality I have chosen does not include taking part in the negativity of those around me and the culture in which I live.

We are connected to everything in the Universe and beyond, so when we raise our energy level as much as possible, the vibration of everything else is elevated as well.

I have opted to take part in the Process of Conscious Human Evolution that is ushering us into The New Era. As we venture forth into uncharted realms, where thoughts manifest quickly, it is essential to become impeccable, both in thought and deed.

Life occurs seamlessly when we tune into the infinite supply of guidance available to us in the form of *perception* and *feelings*. When we increase our level of awareness, by using perception and then follow up by listening to our feelings, everything is as it should be. When we do not, we learn lessons.

There is a channeled source of guidance available to each of us, a divine flow of energy from our Higher

Selves and beyond, intended to help us through life. Once we learn to take notice of this guidance, and then go a step further and begin to listen to it, we become aware that any resistance we are experiencing, melts away and the path becomes clear.

We are multi-dimensional beings.

We are defined by the combination of physical, emotional, etheric, and spiritual aspects of our existence, as well as all the other parts that are outside the scope of our rational understanding, both here on Earth, on other planets, solar systems, and dimensions.

Dimensions can be large and expansive, stretching out to the far reaches of the universe, or they may exist in realms that are smaller than our mind can comprehend.

I am not conscious of every lifetime I have experienced, perhaps there have been many. Nor am I aware of every aspect of my multi-dimensional existence, but I have become aware of many things along the way. This knowing comes to me as I place my focus inward towards the essence of my being, allowing my higher consciousness to expand. Answers to everyday questions, important life decisions, and changes to belief systems come to me, as necessary. The

Garden of Eden is not a geographical place, it is a way of life that is of our own making.

Channeling the New Paradigm

We are evolving into an expanded paradigm, The New Era. As we do, we let go of beliefs that no longer serve us, and have been lingering around for ages. By holding on to outdated ways of thinking, we make it more difficult to change.

Furthermore, old beliefs, prevent us from reaching the higher levels of consciousness we are pursuing. We update our computer operating systems on a regular basis, yet we still practice religions, and hold on to customs that are now archaic.

The origins of many cultural beliefs, held as true by many, are often inaccurate, obscure, and based on misinterpreted translations of ancient texts. Why are our accepted beliefs based on old ideas that have not changed for hundreds of years? Are we incapable of wisdom?

The world has evolved over the centuries, and now we require innovative ideas that reflect our emerging consciousness. It is time to grow into a reality that is more fantastic than anything else we have known. As we increase our awareness of our place in the universe, we gradually enter higher levels of consciousness, ones that resonate with the heartbeat of all that is.

We are in uncharted territory.

There are no templates or references for the new vibrations we are experiencing. Fortunately for us, fresh information, pertinent to the currently evolving human consciousness, is available to everyone. It is brought through by us, the Earthly Light Beings that we have become, dedicated to bringing the messages of Angelic Beings and Ascended Masters.

Just as the ancients had their wisdom and knowledge, so do we. The insights of antiquity are beautiful and spiritually invigorating, and for all we know, might have been channeled in the same manner and from the same Luminous Beings that are sending us pertinent information from the Higher Realms today, through the channels of our age.

We are living in exceptional times, but even though we have assimilated many traditional concepts, we must be willing to imagine the impossible, step beyond the apparent, and integrate what were previously called miracles into our ordinary reality, if we are to advance beyond the mundane existence that has existed on our planet for ages.

We are venturing beyond science and the empirical process that demands proof using the five senses and embracing our inherent wisdom and intuitive skills. By doing so, we realize that we are much more than we ever thought we could be.

The Higher Self

As we read a book and focus on the content, there is another part of us that knows we are reading a book. This is our Higher Self, our Soul, the true essence of our being, or whatever name we wish to use. It is the part of us that was with us before we entered this incarnation, and will move on to the next phase when we leave.

The Higher Self is the part of us that sings our unique note, which resonates with the universe, and defines us.

If this still seems a bit vague or difficult to grasp, let me put it another way. Imagine being at the market and you cannot decide what to buy for dinner. As you are choosing what to eat, there is a dialogue happening. You are thinking to yourself and having a conversation in your mind, or in some cases verbally. But to whom are you actually speaking?

Yes, that is the Higher Self, the part of us that we talk to and communicate with in our mind. We know, that *it* knows, what we should have for dinner, and everything else that pertains to us, even those things we do not think we know. When we listen to our Higher Self, and trust the answers we receive, things go well. When we do not listen, we usually end up thinking, *I knew I should have…*

The Higher Self is the part of us connected with the Higher Source of Everything. Higher than what, we might ask? Higher than the vibration we are currently experiencing in our Third Dimensional everyday realities and rational, logical thought processes, which we were taught are the ultimate source of wisdom and knowledge in life, but in reality, separates us from our true source of guidance.

However, there are ways that we can reconnect to Source, but first we must have the intention to do so. Instead of following the crowd, doing, and thinking what everyone else does, we can begin consulting our intuition, a discipline that we must reclaim and re-develop.

The way to do this is by practicing. As we become more accustomed to consulting our own wisdom, we receive guidance in the form of *feelings*. When we trust our ability to perceive our feelings, we are moving with the rhythm of life. Everything that lives, has knowingness. We can see this by observing nature, with its order and synchronistic, fractal patterns. This natural rhythm is part of our consciousness, because we are part of nature.

Our Higher Self has an impeccable source of guidance.

Our Higher Self has all the knowledge and wisdom we require while here on Earth. The extent of this information that we can access is directly proportional to our Light Quotient. Therefore, the Process of Conscious Human Evolution, or the Ascension Process, is the most important aspect of our lives.

Once we consciously tap into our Higher Self and open the channel so that the connection is stronger, we have a source of impeccable guidance that allows us to observe miracles.

Many people do not believe that visions of Angels, Ascended Masters, and other elements of mystical occurrences that took place in days gone by, can happen in present day life. How unfortunate it would be if we could not experience anything outside the realm of ordinary reality. Life would be very boring. But that is not the case. We can venture into the unknown and find out what is on the other side of the veil.

This is the best of times. Every day we can bring increased Light into the world, and thereby raise the vibration of humanity. When have we ever had the opportunity to evolve into a crystalline cellular structure and a new physical form?

It is easy to look around and see who is flexible and who is rigidly resisting. The choice is ours, we can align with our ego, and have a challenging time, or we can once again connect with our Higher Selves and shed the layers of dense energy that will keep us down.

It is an easy choice, but for those who cannot or will not embrace change, it is nearly impossible. The funny part, if there is a funny part, is that even if we resist change, it is occurring all around us.

We are on the journey of a lifetime. Many souls have incarnated to Earth at this time to take part in the Process of Conscious Human Evolution, and we are among them. So, we may as well start enjoying the experience as much as possible. The NOW in which we are living will be looked back upon by future generations as the re-emergence of humanity from the Dark Ages into the Light, the same way we look back upon the Age of Enlightenment as the time when the injustices of the church gave way to reason. In *The New Era*, the limitations of pure reason will give way to the expansion of consciousness.

The current system here on Earth is not working for many, but for others is the catalyst for change. Intention is the key and the ticket for the fantastic journey that is available to all who are willing to take the giant leap of faith into the unknown. The rewards make it all worthwhile.

The Process of Ascension

In old-fashioned hot air balloons, the more weight that was dropped from the basket, the higher it ascended. The same is true for our Ascension process. As we let go of heavier, denser energies, that no longer serve us, we naturally raise our consciousness.

It is no longer necessary to spend years working through the trauma and pain, of events we have experienced. We can just let go of past, painful events, thereby sending denser energies we have been holding on to, into the Violet Flame of Purification to be transmuted into the pure Light from whence they came. After that, we can fill the places that were once dark, with Light.

Let it go.

As we continue on the path of Conscious Human Evolution, we realize how fortunate we are to live a new phase of human development. Many of us are writing, blogging, texting, and discussing the amazing changes that are materializing in our everyday life. No longer is the Ascension Process the belief of only a few, it is the beginning of what will one day be the new reality here on Earth, not for just the ones who know it now, but for all.

Ascension Symptoms

As we continue to release lower energies, many of us are experiencing Ascension Symptoms. These uncomfortable feelings occur at various times, depending on the physical and emotional state of the individual, time of year, astrological circumstances, weather, and events in our lives. The difficulty we face as we experience these physical expressions of the energetic changes in our light bodies, is how to handle ourselves in these situations, since we have few references.

What exactly are Ascension Symptoms? As we ascend, raising our vibration, our energy and physical bodies are adjusting, to barely perceptible higher dimensions. Of course, our physical bodies stay in the vibration of the Third Dimension, but at a different level to which we are accustomed.

To give an example, when we were children, we lived in the world, but not as we do now. We lived in the dimension of a child, and it was as valid a reality as any other. The same is true now that we are in our adult world, and as we evolve, we move into other frequencies of that world. Just as our bodies grew when we were children, our Light Bodies grow as spiritual seekers.

Each level of vibration has its own reality, and as we move through the different mini-dimensions that blend together and fade into each other, our physical and energetic bodies change, usually imperceptibly, but occasionally the Quantum Leap is greater and becomes noticeable in the Third Dimension.

Those are the times when we have AHA moments and feel exceptionally wonderful. These blissful occurrences lift us higher than we have been, but then we return to our normal state...or do we? The answer is *no*, we do not. As we become inspired, we are lifted. In the afterglow, we remain a bit higher than before.

Time to Nurture Ourselves

These types of experiences are the pleasing part of the process, the ones that leave us feeling we have truly accomplished a bit of personal and spiritual growth, and we feel better. However, it is important to understand that while these lofty feelings are occurring, other processes are also happening. We are detoxifying as we release old thought patterns and beliefs that no longer serve us and letting go old energy lodged in our physical form.

In addition, as we relinquish lower energies, our light bodies must adjust to the new ways of thinking we now embrace. This naturally affects our physical condition. The body, which has infinite wisdom, also makes the necessary adjustments under the command of the cells, which are responding to the impulses they are receiving from the brain. As a result, we feel exhausted, have aches and pains, experience anxiety, become impatient, and basically do not feel the way we think we should after doing all that energy work, but it is all the energy work that causes us to go through the changes, and it is the same energy work that will make us bounce back.

A few years ago, I took Metatronic Keys III, an online class with James Tyberonn. For a few weekends I attended sessions, and had some amazing, enlightening experiences from these classes, which I highly recommend.

Then came the Full Moon of the Emerald Ray and the pull of Mercury in retrograde. For the next two days I found I had no energy to do anything but sleep and eat. In the days following, as I honored my need for nurturing, I felt renewed, an improved version of myself.

As we go through these processes, finding ourselves in states of consciousness that we have not yet experienced, we are at the lower level of a higher dimension, and we have released a significant amount of old energy to arrive there. We must then replenish our level of Life Force Energy with Light. During this time, we may feel depleted, and that is part of what we call Ascension Symptoms.

It is important to nurture ourselves and return to the basics as we begin new phases in our spiritual development. We can focus on our heart center, exist within the realm of Love, regard everything and everyone, including ourselves, objectively and gently, and embrace Love as our primary focus.

This is important:

As we ascend and then re-visit the most fundamental teachings of our spiritual learning, we can experience them with a new and improved consciousness. We can also express gratitude for our progress, knowing that all that we have done will benefit not only us, but the entire world. As we grow into our new Light Bodies, the discomfort will vanish, and we will realize the Divine Beings of Light that we are.

Knowing

Many of us are reluctant to acknowledge the validity of innovative ideas unless they receive the blessing of science. This diminishes our intuitive powers and natural wisdom, to the realm of having little significance or importance. By doing so, we are declaring ourselves hardly capable of knowing something, unless scientifically trained people review, study, and prove it is valid.

Modern science has only been around for a brief time in our history, so why is it the ultimate source of truth for all our ideas and beliefs? How did people survive, some in societies more advanced than our own, without science?

I find Quantum Physics fascinating, so I do not wish to criticize scientists, but they are not divine. They are using a systematic process to validate theories that do not need proof for anyone who has faith in life and a connection with their intuitive wisdom.

In the end, I must praise science with the highest regard, for leading the way to the enhancement of our lives through the development and refinement of technology. Without them we would be living in a world of physical struggle. On the other hand, if we had relied on our knowing instead, we might even be much farther along.

Scientific theories are only true within the boundaries of a system of deductive method. Suppose there are those who believe that we can step out of time and not take part. If I am late for work one day and decide not to look at the clock, but rather measure time the way I wish, in other words, slow time down so that I am not late, then is time really time? Does it really work the way we believe it does? Try it some time, it's fun.

> *We know not what else we can achieve,*
> *if we are willing to dare to dream.*

Dr. Masaru Emoto, author of *Hidden Messages in the Water*, states that you can look at a cloud and choose to erase it from the sky. If you do, is that cloud still there for someone else? It is possible, but you must believe you can do it. I like to look at clouds and see the shapes they take, so I am not inclined to practice erasing them.

If George Lucas can conceive of the powers of the Jedi, then how can they not exist, if it is the thought itself that creates the reality? Since there are those, including myself, who have claimed to erase clouds and alter time, then what is REALLY true? Is anything absolutely true or is truth only what most of us decide is true?

The Jedi learned the path to immortality. If we can conceive of such a thing, then why can't it be possible? Are we any more real than the characters in works of fiction? Was there a time when humans lived at a different vibration, one of peace and harmony? If we can envision it, then it must be possible. What if it still exists in a parallel reality? When we look in a wooded area, sometimes we can see beings, not with our eyes, but with our senses. Is all art and literature the reality of another dimension coming through to the artist's mind?

Don't worry, I'm just trying to illustrate that we can *think outside the box*, and to demonstrate how we can experience reality in a different way. For we know not what else we can achieve if we are willing to dare to dream.

Think of what it must have been like when the belief, that the Earth is really round instead of flat, emerged into the collective consciousness. Imagine how happy you would be if you discovered something that big. I choose not to set my sights any lower.

We live in a world where technology is developing and evolving continuously. There are software programmers writing code and hackers breaking into those programs, so that the developers must create even more advanced software, to fight off the hackers. It goes on and on. Each idea is a steppingstone to the next level.

Unlike technology, our cultural belief systems, have barely changed in thousands of years. We call them traditions and think they are quaint and precious, but our values must also evolve, or they become irrelevant to the vibration of the life we are living.

For this reason, significant numbers of people are losing interest in organized religion, and others are having to struggle to hold on to their old ways, even to fight wars over them. These principles extend to all areas of our lives, including who we choose for a life partner, the attitude we have towards others, our thoughts on bringing up our children, our views about the universe, and our concept of divinity.

If we do not take the time to figure out what we believe, blindly accepting the conventions of the society in which we live, we will be rendered less powerful.

All knowledge resides within us.

We assume that we only know what we learn or are exposed to, but if that is true then how is it, we can remember what happened in past lifetimes? In fact, where do new ideas come from?

When unfamiliar information comes directly to us, without any apparent outside influence, we generally assume we are inspired, downloading, or even channeling. But nothing is really new, only forgotten or entering our consciousness as we raise our vibration.

All knowledge resides within us, therefore when we have a great new idea, it is not something we thought of or created. It is only a remembrance, stored in our etheric mind, which has always been there, but was filed away in the *other incarnations* section.

This is not to say that we cannot receive inspiration and information from outside sources, as in the case of channeled information, for we most certainly can and do, but as we resonate with these new ideas it becomes apparent that we are only becoming re-acquainted with what we once knew.

When we become aware of the possibility that we know more than we think, and that on some levels we actually know everything, we are able to start manifesting what we call miracles, or put another way, that which is outside the realm of what we believe is possible. Then, as we continue to expand what we consider to be achievable, we start to create the abundance we desire.

The way to gain access to the infinite source of everything is to practice. When we cannot think of the solution to a question, we can just ask for guidance from our Higher Selves, Angels, or Ascended Masters. When I am not feeling inspired to write, I surrender to embrace the quiet time, and before long the inspiration comes in an outpouring of thoughts.

I do not doubt my intuitive mind. Once I get the inkling that something might be true, I use discernment, by passing it through the filter of my feelings, to decide if I believe it to be so. The I allow myself to *know* what I cannot rationally have proven with conventional methods.

The logical system of thinking, in which we have placed our confidence for eons, is now becoming outdated, and functions too slowly to keep up with the changes that are occurring on Earth at this time. Remember, everything we need to know, we already know, so when someone says *you are a know it all*, just say, *I know*.

Celestial Events

Throughout the ages, people have honored the Sun and Moon cycles as markers of essential sacred geometrical aspects of the passage of life on Earth. As true humans, our paths are interwoven into these cycles. Eternally reoccurring events, such as phases of the Moon, eclipses, equinoxes, and solstices, unlike various religious holidays, are indisputably the same for everyone. It makes clear sense for us to focus on that which is simple and undeniable.

We may not all agree on religion, politics, or even what kind of pizza topping we like, but we do know that the seasons exist. They do not necessarily coincide with our present-day calendars, since seasons vary from one geographic location to another, but perhaps this is a good reason for finding a truer approach to the passage of time. We can observe the degree of the angle of the sunlight that shines on us, or position of the moon at various times of the year, and this cannot be disputed.

Holidays of organized religions were created as a substitute and alternative to the Earth, Sun, and star-based celebrations, but the Earth is our Goddess and her cycles are our proper times of celebration. She sustains us in every way, supplying us with food and water, without which we would not continue to be alive.

In addition, she re-charges us with the crystalline energy that radiates from deep within her core and from the dodecahedral grid that surrounds her. In our multidimensional existence, we need food in many forms, and the Earth supplies us with all that we require. She is our provider, our pharmacy, and our comfort, giving us shelter, warmth, oxygen, and beauty.

We can show gratitude for her blessings through the observance of her cycles, which are obvious to us in the form of physical changes in our environment. These changes are also essential to our well-being, allowing us to be quiet and still in the low months, excited and hopeful in the anticipation of spring, fervent and passionate in the season of warmth, and thankful and balanced in the times of plenty.

Our celebrations of these periods reflect the characteristics of the seasons, and facilitate our participation in the natural cycles of our lives. Even when living in an urban environment, we can connect with the Earth and observe the natural changes that take place like clockwork.

The Autumnal Equinox is a time of plenty, gratitude, and balance. We eat the foods of the season, surround ourselves with warm colors, admire the fiery shades of the leaves on the trees, and bask in the richness of life that we experience during this time of year. Giving thanks, allows us the pleasure of enjoying the abundance of living.

Even if we live in a warm climate, we can experience the changes. As we turn back towards the natural rhythm of life, we become a reflection of it, balanced and filled with joy.

During the winter we rest, sleep, and live from the fruits of our labors. We keep the lights on longer to counter the increased darkness, and seek out the security and comfort of home, friends, and family. It is a time for reflection and slowness.

Spring arrives and the Vernal Equinox marks the last day that is shorter than the night. Rebirth abounds and each day is like a painting that has more color added to it than the day before. We smell the perfume in the air and adore the flowers when they make their appearance. Once more we hear the sound of the birds chirping their messages of renewal, and again feel the hint of warmth as winter makes its retreat.

Summer warms us so that we can shed our outer garments and feel the sun on our skin. It is a time for recreation or re-creating a world where we can live closer to nature. The Earth sends us gifts of fresh fruits, vegetables, and plenty.

Celebrate the natural cycles of Life.

When we relish the seasons as sacred, they provide balance in our lives and encourage us to be grateful for all that life on Earth has to offer. We will not be not afraid and full of anticipation for what we fear, and will not see the world as a place in need of healing and the environment as damaged. Instead, we can envision the world as the wonder it is, and the air, water, sky, and forests as perfectly how they should be.

Our world is a reflection of us, but the Earth is not a victim of humankind, she is strong and vibrant and has been here through many civilizations, some far more advanced than ours. She will endure, as will we.

As we follow our journey of Conscious Human Evolution, we can believe in ourselves and in Gaia. She is our mother and sustainer, and it is up to us to honor and cherish her. It is from her that we live and breathe, and it is she who loves us unconditionally. We can unite with her in so many ways, even if we must walk on concrete. Watching a TV show about the natural world can connect us with the energy of Mother Earth, if we have the intention. She will know and send her loving, nourishing energy to re-vitalize and renew us.

It is only fear that separates us from the Source of all creation and holds us captive in the clutches of those who have instilled that trepidation within us. Instead, we can nurture, pamper, and love ourselves. Our world will reflect our actions.

We are of the Earth, powerful, vital, kind, and Divine, nothing can harm us. As we tune into the vibration of trees, animals, clouds, and water, we resonate with a place where we are calm and safe. As we become part of the real world, the natural world, we become part of a perfect creation. In this place we find everything we desire, coming to us effortlessly and freely, as we live connected to the cycles of life that continue in fractal patterns and exquisite designs. We are also of that lineage. When we see the beauty of the creation that is us, it is amazing.

Life is a dance - learn to move with the rhythm.

The mother that adores us, Terra, eternally fashions the beauty of our world. The Earth is not just a planet, she lives, breathes, loves, creates, and gives birth to her young then watches them grow. She is the Divine Mother and sustainer of us all, and we must learn once again to return the Love to her, and to appreciate the gifts she has for us.

It's Time

Each moment exists once in an eternity. How we experience those moments is by lining them up in sequential order and calling it time. Time is how we organize, group, and clump together the possibilities we have chosen, are choosing, and plan to choose from the infinite options available to us.

Time is not an absolute truth, it is a practical, useful system we have created to allow us to have an orderly, linear view of reality in the Third Dimension. We are not actually moving ahead through time; it only appears that we are because that is the view of time we have embraced. Every moment matters. Therefore, it is important for us to be consciously aware of all that we are creating, because the fruits of the present will be dumped in our laps any second.

With this Quantum view, there is no past or future, only countless situations of consciousness that we *have* used or *will* use. As we participate in a co-creative process with Universal Intelligence, we create events with our individual and group thought forms. The past is like a big filing system that we can refer to, when we wish to recall instances of consciousness that we have experienced. Because of this, we sometimes get a feeling something will happen, or we think of someone and they call us. The event already exists, it just has not arrived into our *now* yet, but we are connected to it, since we beckoned it.

Oh, the cleverness of it all.

As Wallace Wattles said quite simply, there is a thinking substance that permeates and surrounds all things, and it is from this intelligent substance that matter is created. However, the time has come to expand this principle further. In stating that the intelligent substance is everywhere, and also nowhere, we must define what the intelligence is.

Since it is permeating and surrounding everything and is even the substance of what we call *nothing*, we must conclude that it is what many call by names such as Spirit, The Force, the Divine, or whatever makes us feel comfortable. We want everyone to be happy.

So, when it is said that Spirit is everywhere, it is true, and the infinite intelligence in the universe is *from* it, as it expresses itself in the form of consciousness, the creative force, and the source of matter from which everything is made. So basically, we are all swimming around in a sea of divine substance that creates and sustains us. Oh, the cleverness of it all…

A Divine Life

Anything that transcends our rational thought processes is difficult to define in words, especially when it is a force greater than we are. The very act of trying to conceptualize a deity, just to give ourselves comfort, is an exercise in futility, for as soon as we describe what that divine being is, we miss the mark.

Many are living under the illusion that they are separate from the Divine. They have taken the most important aspect of life and placed it into a physical form, separate from them, thereby removing themselves from the most fundamental part of their existence, and keeping it hidden beyond their reach, somewhere in the sky.

The same way we may have become somewhat estranged from our Higher Selves; we can also become disconnected from divinity. We entered this world as a spark of divine creation, why then would we dissect ourselves into pieces and give some of them to a being from whom we must ask for little bits of what already belongs to us?

Instead, what we can do with our rational minds, is have a growing personal relationship with ourselves and become more aware of our limitless possibilities.

Once we define, we lose the divine.

If we define a divine being as *all that is*, then how can we worship an image or an idea? Shouldn't we believe in everyone and everything? The concept and worship of external celestial deities has been going on for so long that it has become truth and reality, but the time has come to re-evaluate and update our belief systems. Only then can we truly experience a divine life.

Religion is often a controversial topic, because individual beliefs can become easily offended. Although I have never understood why, if someone genuinely believes in something, he or she should take offence by what another person says about it.

Our spiritual practices should provide us with the most happiness in life; therefore, it puzzles me why religion is so exceedingly serious and solemn instead of joyous and uplifting.

I am reluctant to embrace principles that separate people, so this makes it difficult for me to take part in organized religion. Instead, I prefer to believe in the celebration of the Divine in every living part of creation and all that defines it.

Our beliefs are correct for us, for they will either serve us or teach us, but it is important to decide what we truly believe, even if our attitudes change over time.

A good starting point for the examination of our core principles, is the realization that we are not all born sinful beings. If we lived in a perfect paradise and knew that the only thing we had to do to remain there was not to eat a particular piece of fruit from a special tree, does it seem likely that we would? I mean, come on, and to make matters worse, it is the fault of a woman that we are all suffering, because she tempted the man to eat from the forbidden apple tree. Excuse me, but didn't he know better, if such a tale could possibly be true? Wouldn't it have been prudent for him to say, Eve, let's have pears for dinner, dear.

Yet, we speak of this incident as if it actually happened in recorded history. I would sooner believe that the fall of humanity occurred when inequality between man, woman, and nature began, resulting in an imbalance on earth. Now it is time to find the way back to a world based on respect for life.

We are here on Earth to live a Divine life. Does it sound like a fairy tale? Perhaps it seems so distant that it will never be part of our reality in this day and age, and instead must be classified as a state of mind, only available to mystics and men sitting in caves in the Himalayas or on mountain tops in Peru. However, a divine life is our legacy, the only thing that stands between living it and not, is our vibration.

No matter what kind of life we had up until this moment, our divine life can start right now. The first step is to believe that it is possible to live a divine life and then we must have the intention to make it our own. See, that was easy, now wasn't it? We have already gotten over the biggest hurdle of all, changing what we accept as truth.

A Divine life begins with how we view and treat ourselves, practicing Love and honor in all aspects of life, and not allowing even one moment or action to compromise the integrity of the standard of excellence we have established for ourselves.

We can begin by showing gratitude for what we have already received, loving our life and those in it, caring for our body, and enjoying all the activities that fill our day. When we do this, we are ensuring that our life will always be lifted to the standard we have set for ourselves.

When we Love our job, it provides us with the income that supports the lifestyle we desire. When we Love our friends, they are the mirrors in which we see our character. When we Love our enemies, they teach us lessons and allow us to strengthen our values. Then we can Love ourselves for living a Divine life.

To live a divine life, we must embrace the concept of Divinity, and the way that it manifests everyday. We are all connected, or simply put, we are all in this together. Each of us is just as important and essential to life as everyone else, so we must give each person the same Love and respect. That is the essence of divinity, to see that everything that exists is an expression and a reflection of the Divine.

To continue living a Divine life, we must look upon everything with Love. This means accepting others the way they are and allowing them to fulfill their life's purpose, just as we do ours. At times this can be extremely difficult, especially when we have the desire to help someone because we have already learned what they have not, but we should not attempt to impose our wisdom on others, or deprive them of their lessons. Instead, we can be an example and a Bringer of Light. By doing so, we will be providing others with the opportunity to see us shine.

Life is an occasion, rise to it.

Loving, means viewing others without judgment, criticism, or ridicule. We might have been the same way as they are, at another part of our journey. Just because we have gone farther, does not mean we are better or wiser, it is only an indication of the current vibration of our Light Body. There are other moments when our vibration might have been much different and in other simultaneously existing dimensions, things might even be reversed.

When living a Divine Life, our thoughts towards others remain positive, uplifting, and impeccable, just the same as our words. Changing judgmental, assumptive ideas, which are the result of living in a competitive society where everyone is expected to give up much of their identity and adopt the beliefs of the culture, can be difficult. However, with practice, we find that doing so is refreshing and vitalizing.

Perceiving others with unconditional love, changes our world and attracts people who are on the same journey as ourselves, some are farther along and others by our side, but it is all as it should be.

As we step into a Divine Life on our journey of Conscious Human Evolution, we are moving into a place where life is good, and all is well. We do not see a world that is damaged, but instead we see a place where there is potential for us to raise our consciousness. After all, we live in a universe that functions perfectly on an infinitely grand scale, so we certainly cannot assume that events that are occurring here on Earth, will upset the impeccable workings of the cosmos.

Our mission now is to let go of the current reality with which we no longer resonate and change our thoughts and beliefs to higher vibrating ones, allowing us to gracefully evolve into higher aspects of ourselves. This transition is inevitable, already in progress, and cannot be postponed for another day.

As we begin to look at the world as a place of wonder and perfection, filled with plants, animals, minerals, and people that are all on the same guided, evolutionary path, we see the beauty in everyone and everything.

Each person was once a little baby that was cooed and cuddled. That being is still inside their body with a perfect, loving spirit just like ours. Our higher dimensional self knows only truth and unconditional Love. As we connect to this part of us, and make it our intention to be surrounded by the energy of Love and Light, then we are living a Divine Life.

Changing Our Past

Many of us have had the experience of reflecting on past events of our lives and wishing that they might have occurred differently. Of course, we all know that this is not possible...or is it? We assume that once something has happened it is set in stone; most people do not even question that concept.

All the events that occurred in the past have brought us to where we are now. So, if we are happy, we can look back at our lives and realize that everything we experienced, was part of our path to happiness. Now that we have learned the lessons that contributed to making us happy, wouldn't it be nice to change a disagreeable event into a more pleasant memory?

Whatever happened in the past was the result of possible choices we made at the time. The remaining choices, which we never chose, still exist in the realm of infinite possibilities, which reside in the infinite consciousness. We can change what happened, by thinking back and re-constructing it into a pleasant memory. Even if the event itself was disagreeable, if we learned something, or evolved because of it, we can focus on that aspect of it instead of the displeasing part.

The old memory will eventually fade away and the new perception of it will take its place. Reality is a point of view, and we are the ones who can change it. It is possible to re-program the past to be as we wish.

Why should we saddle ourselves with painful memories? Isn't the goal of psychoanalysis and energy work healing the past and changing it from something that causes us pain or difficulty, into an event that no longer affects us? We can do the same thing ourselves with our own mind.

There is one essential step in the process and that is *forgiveness*. The act of forgiving someone who hurt us, breaks the bond that connects us to that action and replaces it with grace. Forgiving someone does not mean that we forget what happened, but by doing so we are no longer the recipient of the injurious feelings.

In any situation there are always at least one participant, so it is necessary to forgive ourselves for our part in holding on to pain. This must occur wholeheartedly for it to be true forgiveness. When we do this, without placing blame, feelings of purification and peace will be our reward.

We can take this exercise back to memories of our childhood, to change events that made us unhappy, the bully at school, the friends who refused to play with us, the things we all did as selfish children.

We have chosen this particular timeline of the past, present, and future as our reality, but it is not the only one. It is wonderful and magical when we become aware of our ability to transform energy and create a life full of magnificent experiences, both in the past and those yet to come.

We Are Stars

Enough of Darwin and Newton, we must relinquish their theories and reach out into the unknown for new truths. Modern science was in its infancy in 1859 when the Origin of Species was published. This is exemplified by Viennese physician Ignaz Semmelweis, Darwin's contemporary, who proposed his cutting-edge theory that physicians, who had been working on cadavers, should wash their hands before delivering babies. For his contribution to medicine, he was later declared insane for his ideas and committed to a mental asylum where he died.

We are grateful to these men for the giant steps they took in their time, but now we are embarking upon the Quantum Age, and we require new ideas and beliefs to move us forward into the higher dimensions that are rapidly approaching.

Darwin and Newton were great men in their time, but this is *our* time. Our scientific progress has sped up exponentially in the last few decades, due to easily accessible global communication, allowing us to see rapid changes.

Mr. Darwin's notion that we evolved from the apes, was logical based on the data available at the time, but there were other factors that were not considered. First, we do not necessarily live only once and then go reside for all eternity in Heaven or Hell. This is a myth, no more valid than the Greek myths of Mt. Olympus and Hades.

Even today, what we believe about the time before our birth and what happens after we die, or even if we are supposed to die, is only based on what we have been taught by the religious and scientific schools of the day. Logical and faith-based beliefs are not absolute, they can change. Over time, many Gods become one God and new theories invalidate the old ones.

In the current, innovative scientific thought of today, it is becoming accepted, by those who are willing to step outside of the proverbial box, that contrary to Darwin's Theory of Evolution, we are not slaves to our DNA structure. In fact, we can alter our DNA by changing our beliefs. The science of Epigenetics has determined that the cell wall is its actual brain. It responds to the electromagnetic signals it receives through receptors from our thoughts and our environment.

Newtonian Physics is based on duality, meaning that an object is either *here* or *there*. However, we have now promoted ourselves into the realm of Quantum Physics where much more is possible. We are finding that molecules can be in two places at once and even disappear and reappear. But as advanced as we may think we are today, our belief systems may also one day be studied in a Mythology class at some University, for credit towards a degree.

Most of us have lived many lives. Some of us can even remember other incarnations and how we are still connected to them. I recall living in the same place on Earth that I live now, but in a different time. I have recollections of other lifetimes in Glastonbury, England, Atlantis, Orion, and even the Deep South. So, if I lived here in a different lifetime as a Native American, how can I determine who my ancestors are? I have many and they might be scattered all over the planet, in other galaxies, or even in other dimensions.

In addition, and this is a big one, we are certainly not the first civilization to exist on earth. There have been others that have come and gone, some with ends that could have been better, but the origin of our species is not a protozoa or an amoeba, it is much grander, no offense given to the one-celled.

We were brought here to this planet from the far reaches of the Universe. We have ancestors on many Star systems and galaxies. The beings who are our true cousins and relatives remember us and watch over us. They are here among us and eventually we will unite with them. The *powers that be* do not want us to know this, so they try, with all their might, to make us fear anything or anyone originating from places other than Earth.

We came from the stars.

More and more people are channeling beings from other dimensions and star systems, using their natural telepathic abilities to connect with those who have been waiting for us to reach a higher vibration that will allow us to communicate with our distant neighbors, those who seeded us here long ago and are more advanced than we can ever remember being.

They built massive structures with mathematical accuracy which cannot be duplicated by modern day engineers. They developed crystal generators capable of producing more clean energy than we can even dream of creating with our current, comparatively feeble fossil fuel generating stations and atomic reactors. Think of what they accomplished, being able to travel from planet to planet, even through solar systems and dimensions. Compare this to how far we, as a civilization, are from being able to carry out such feats.

There are kind and loving beings in the universe, and we can learn from them. We are stars, we came from the stars, and when we rise above the dense thought patterns that have been inflicted upon us, we will then rise like stars again and shine our Light, so that others can see there still is a Light.

Conscious Human Evolution

Evolution took place gradually in the past, compared to the rate at which the planet is currently changing. Today's world is filled with artificial substances that have contributed to alterations in our bodies. Pollution, pharmaceuticals, global warming, and the vibrations of humans, constantly living in a stressful state, all affect our physical and energetic conditions in ways we cannot know.

We do not even look the same as people did a hundred years ago, but it is not only changes in style that produce modifications in individual countenances, it is the sum total of the evolutionary transformations that have occurred over time.

Human evolution is a sensitive topic, as we are programmed to believe that we are the absolute highest illustration of a life form that can exist. In fact, each of us is changing every moment, therefore there is no need for judgment, since every step of the process is appropriate and perfect to get us to the next phase.

Conscious Human Evolution has also been going on for ages, but it has exponentially advanced in the last two decades or so, partly because of technology. We can communicate with one another now more than ever, sharing contemporary ideas and information that facilitates and accelerates Spiritual growth.

Traditionally the term evolution refers to perceptible physical changes in species, but currently we use it to refer to the spiritual or emotional growth of individuals, which is a vague, immeasurable concept.

As our vibration increases, we enter higher states of consciousness. For example, we might respond to the actions and comments of others by taking it personally, but at a higher level we can realize that their actions have nothing to do with us at all, and they are only expressing something about themselves through their interaction with us. Often the other person is not even aware of what is going on, but from a higher point of view it becomes clear to us.

The process of spiritual growth can be likened to stepping out of the fog and seeing things that were there all along but were not visible to us. It can be a slow process for some, and for others it can be instantaneous, depending on the person and their experiences in life.

It is possible that evolutionary growth will not happen for some in their current lifetime and an individual will live in the fog, doing the same things repeatedly, never changing, even when presented with the opportunity to transform.

The more enlightened person knows that we are all equal, but that others may not be ready to undergo the personal growth process. It may not be part of their journey, but even so, their path is just as valid as ours. What we must remember is that since we are all connected, the world cannot exist without them or us, we are all part of the whole.

My primary focus in life is Conscious Human Evolution, the voyage of spiritual growth. However, enlightenment is not an actual goal, it is a process. We do not reach enlightenment and exist at the highest point with nowhere else to go. On the human, Third Dimensional level there might be a ceiling, but at that point an infinite number of dimensions await our discovery.

We are each a grain of sand in an endless desert and a drop of water in an infinite ocean. There is no such thing as achieving enlightenment and sitting on a cloud for all eternity with the other Angels and Masters. Instead, there is a never-ending process, endowed with a goal of continuation and co-creation.

When we place ourselves on that path, then we are Enlightened, and as we continue, we become more so. But let us not try to measure the heights to which we feel we are ascending, let us savor every moment of the journey in this lifetime, for it is a precious gift and a miracle. Let us be in awe of it.

The Law of Attraction

Like attracts like. We resonate with certain people, places, food, colors, and just about everything. When the vibrations of people resonate, they attract, and when they do not, they repel. This is generally accepted and agreed upon by most everyone.

What is not known, is *why* we resonate with another person and why we are attracted to them. Furthermore, what is the real reason we come into conjunction with different people and events?

It is very quantum to say that our compatible vibrations resonate. We accept that this is enough of a reason to form relationships with others, basing our faith on the esoteric explanation that it is *meant to be*. We have so much trust in the process of life that we embrace the higher human and even non-human, beings that we encounter in our mystical road to the higher realms.

What is the real reason that life happens and that the Law of Attraction is part of it? We can observe that the Law is a law, and like attracts like, but we do not know why or for what purpose, we only accept it since something has happened so many times and attained validity, it can safely be called a law.

We embrace our power to create, with passion, knowing that when we value uplifting beliefs and integrity, we are creating that kind of reality. The best part of it all is that *it works,* and not only for us, but for the entire universe. If like did not attract like, and the Law of Attraction was not a reality, nothing would exist. Molecules and atoms would not come together and bond to create matter and life. The Law of Attraction is more than a law, it is the reason for everything.

Even what some call *the void* is subject to the Law. The *void* which some describe as nothingness, is no such thing. If it were so, we could not conceive of it. The fact that we call it anything gives it substance and meaning, and makes it part of reality, so it cannot be the *void*.

What is it then? Well, since you asked, *it is the infinite storehouse of the raw material of creation.* The Law of Attraction is purposefully intended, so that we may have energy, Love, and everything else that is part of the world. It is the true magic of life that transforms and transmutes the raw material of everything that exists, along with consciousness and infinite intelligence, into a concoction that we call reality. Oh, the cleverness...

Synchronicity

Carl Jung defines synchronicity as *meaningful coincidence*. Synchronistic events happen when we are resonating with the diverse vibrations of life. They occur at moments when our thoughts manifest at once in the physical world, without a perceivable time lapse. If we were living to our fullest potential as humans, we would always be manifesting our thoughts when they occur. If this were the case, we would have to be incredibly careful of which thoughts we allow. Synchronistic events happen more frequently, as our awareness of them increases.

We take special notice when these events occur, and we cheerfully tell others about our magical moments. Many of us have had the experience of thinking of someone just as they call on the phone, or we meet them by chance on the street. Occasionally, when I am typing and have music playing in the background, I will hear the word that I am typing at the very moment my fingers are hitting the keys.

Synchronicity is a comma, a pause, occurring when events unfold rhythmically. The timing of something is the same as the timing of something else, and both events harmoniously happen in the same coordinate of our consciousness. This is not what some call coincidence, instead it is a message from the universe, telling us that we are resonating perfectly with the rhythm of life. We can embrace these messages, smiling when they happen, and enjoying the fun of receiving a nudge from beyond our ordinary reality.

The Mystery of Parallel Realities

I researched Stonehenge a fair bit before my amazing tour of Sacred Britain in 2012, with the Earth-Keeper group, but somehow all the articles I read, fell short of explaining what I saw when I arrived. Looking at the stones, it seemed as though I was glimpsing something from another dimension, that had somehow slipped through a veil and had become visible.

Some people claim the stones circle was built to serve as a calendar, a religious site, or even a place for sacrifices to the Gods. Those who built Stonehenge, and other Neolithic sites, are described as primitive, heathen nature-worshippers. Although I read many articles about the site before my trip, when I saw Stonehenge in person, none of what I had read made sense to me.

To begin with, the stones are enormous. I doubt that today we could recreate such a grid of rocks that size. Therefore, to attribute the project to a society of people who were not technologically advanced, seems unlikely. All that I had read about the place, written within the confines of current archeological parameters, did not add up.

So then, what is the explanation of how this anomaly of the British landscape came to be where it is? Well, in truth, no one really knows for sure. It has been determined that the stones replicate our solar system on a smaller scale, and are aligned to the shadow of the sun's rising and setting on solstices and equinoxes, but that is not an explanation, it is a description of characteristics of the henge. Perhaps the time has come for us to depend on our own sense of knowing, intuition, feelings, and information, to help us understand Sacred Sites.

Peeking through the veil…

Many believe that Atlantis existed on this planet tens of thousands of years ago. Others claim it is a reality that exists in the future and is made to appear as though it was in the past, so that we may learn not to make the mistakes we attribute to its demise.

It is also said that Atlantean survivors might have created the mystery stone circle. Others claim it was extra-terrestrials, who came to Earth during a time when there was no advanced technology to apprehend them. All these theories are attempts to make sense of the history of the Earth, but we must remember that we are now in the Quantum Age. We know that everything occurs simultaneously, and there is really no past or future, only versions of the present.

An infinite number of realities occur simultaneously, and most importantly, there are aspects of *us* that are taking part in some or all those realities. This is the reason we can remember being in another *lifetime*, not because it is a past life, but because on some level we ARE there.

So, with that said, we can propose that Atlantis is occurring now in its own reality, as we are in this one, neither being more real or more valid than the other. This is an easy concept to express, but one that is difficult to truly comprehend in our Third Dimensional minds.

Back to Stonehenge, as I stood looking at the stones, I could not mentally process their existence as I normally do. There was something unearthly about them, and then it all became clear. They are visible, inter-dimensional aspects of a structure. In other words, they are from another dimension, but we can see them.

Unlike trees, the sky, humans, animals, water, and every other feature of our world, these stones have a different vibration than our normal reality. However, a portion of their energy signature resonates with ours, allowing them to partially manifest *here*, as well as *there*. Because of this, we are magically drawn to them. The large stones of Stonehenge are living beings of the mineral kingdom that succeed in appearing in our reality. Is this why we see Crop circles? What else might be peeking through the veil?

Nothing

There is a thinking stuff from which all things are made, and which, in its original state, permeates, penetrates, and fills the interspaces of the universe. A thought, in this substance, produces the thing that is imaged by the thought. Man can form things in his thought, and, by impressing his thought upon formless substance, can cause the thing he thinks about to be created. In order to do this, man must pass from the competitive to the creative mind; he must form a clear mental picture of the things he wants, and hold this picture in his thoughts with the fixed PURPOSE to get what he wants, and the unwavering FAITH that he does get what he wants, closing his mind against all that may tend to shake his purpose, dim his vision, or quench his faith.

Wallace Wattles

Everything that exists, is formed and defined by the thinking substance, which fills the interspaces of the universe. We call it *consciousness*. It is the stuff from which our thoughts are created and from whence they take form.

Consciousness is all that exists in our reality and all which does not. Consciousness is infinite. It is merely our awareness of it that increases and our Light Quotient increases.

Quantum physics focuses on breaking down matter to the most minuscule particle possible. This may not even be the smallest there is, but only the tiniest our current technology allows us to recognize. No matter how minutely we break down what we call matter, there will always be something surrounding it, giving it form and existence.

When particles are combined by the intelligent consciousness that surrounds them, objects of matter are created. Because of this there are tables, people, trees, cars, animals, and everything else that we have defined as *existing*. That which does not exist we call nothing.

However, by acknowledging *nothing*, we are validating its existence. The undefined space, which we label as meaningless nothingness, which surrounds and permeates through particles of matter, is what gives form and life to everything. It is The Force that the Jedi's revere in *Star Wars*, and rightly so.

What makes us what we are? I do not mean our personalities, but why am I able to sit here at a computer and type? I am a collection of particles, atoms, and molecules that is held together by...? I am held together by *nothing*, and *nothing* works perfectly. All the space that surrounds every unit of the matter that forms me, is what holds me together. The intelligent nothingness that gives me life, is all around me and flows through me. Yoda was right.

All by which I am defined, is all that I am not.

Quantum theory states that electrons, our source of energy and light, jump from one orbit to another. This may seem uneventful at first mention, but there is more to the story. When the electrons reposition from one path to another, they do not pass through space to do so, they only disappear and reappear. Where do they go in between? They go *nowhere*, and that is where they energize. *Nowhere* is where there is nothing, and that is where the source of Light and life resides.

Magic is part of life.

Having said all this, we can now see how silly it is for us to call the source of our Life Force Energy *nothing*, and have it reside *nowhere*. We are so determined to view and define our existence in absolute terms, that we have virtually cut ourselves off from *Source*. How did this happen?

As rationally thinking beings, at some point we began to believe that we must disregard everything that we cannot explain logically. Prior to this, people were aware of the forces in life which could influence and affect transformation. Ooops, did I just define magic? The "M" word is like a weed. We try to stamp it out, but it always grows up between the cracks. We try to cheapen it by reducing it to a form of entertainment, but then along comes Harry Potter and we cannot stop people from loving the idea of magic.

Magic is transformation, and part of life. We can smile at someone and transform his or her face into a smiling one. That is magic. *Nothing*, as we call it, is magic, and that is what gives us form.

The problem is that it is difficult to control people when they become aware that transformation is possible. When we become conscious that we have the power to improve our lives by changing the way we think, then we can choose our own belief systems, realize our own power, discover we can heal our body, mind, and spirit, rise above the system which has taken control here on Earth, and decide to be happy. It is then and only then that external control ends, and personal power takes over.

When we are happy, energized, vitalized, and we know that what they call *nothing* is just as real as what we call *something*. When the *seen* and the *unseen*, the *real* and the *unreal*, *something* and *nothing* become balanced, we create a state of wholeness, fcr it is then that Life Force Energy flows freely through us.

Angels and Ascended Masters

Archangels, Angels, Ascended Masters, Guides, and all higher Beings of Light, exist in their own vibration, just as we do. We, as humans, cannot presume to completely understand their purpose in being, yet we do know that they are willing and able to assist us in a variety of ways, and that it is a true blessing they wish to do so.

Each of these beings has areas of expertise, just as we do, and when we become familiar with their particular talent, it becomes easier to know which Light Being to call upon.

The most important thing to remember when working with our luminescent friends is that they respect our free will. Therefore, it is up to us to call on them when we require their guidance and assistance. Only then will they come into our lives to work with us. It is amazing how almost at once, we can feel their presence when we invoke them.

Angels and Ascended Masters are near.

As we become sensitive to the subtle energy around us, we begin to feel a gentle lightening of the field in our immediate surroundings when the Higher Beings are working with us. They are waiting for us to ask for assistance, so that they may fulfill their purpose, but they cannot take on our responsibilities or achieve personal growth for us.

What they can do, is offer guidance and an etheric cushion so that we may achieve our spiritual goals more easily and gracefully. Even if we do not require specific help with a particular issue, life can be much more fulfilling with the presence of Light Beings. Just reading about them, or even thinking of them, creates a soothing, calming sensation that reminds us of a place that has been forgotten long ago, yet always deeply yearned for.

Angels are waiting to assist us.

Light Beings come to us in a few ways, not just in our thoughts and feelings, but also by sending physical, third-dimensional messages. We can be sure there is a Light Being smiling at our amazement and delight over synchronistic events, which they may have helped to orchestrate. Without them life is mundane and tedious, with them it is magical and mystical.

There is a reason we feel drawn to a certain Archangel or Ascended Master. We may be of the same lineage and destined to work with that Being of Light. As we learn more, we may feel a closer connection with them and even begin to receive clear messages via our thoughts. Over time we can create a relationship with our Archangels, Ascended Masters, Angels, and Guides, that can last a lifetime or longer. Their guidance and assistance are an essential part of the Ascension process, as we head into this new territory.

New Wisdom

Most of us who are consciously involved in the Ascension process, may feel overwhelmed when trying to integrate the information that is coming through daily. As soon as we assimilate a new idea, another one emerges through our intuition and channeling abilities.

Throughout history, most knowledge was shared by word of mouth. Information was not written, neither was it forgotten. As we learn to access information clairvoyantly, we are not limited to the study of ancient techniques for our truths. Many of the teachings of antiquity were the highest form of wisdom in their time, and some still have relevance today. But our task is to remember what once existed and has been forgotten, and at the same time receive knowledge not previously known to us here on Earth.

The vibration of the messages we are bringing in from the higher realms, is compatible with the current energy. Often the messages act as a trigger, producing great strides in our evolutionary paths. The same message can also be relevant at a future time, resonating on a different level with a higher consciousness, inspiring us to an even further advancement in the Ascension process.

Being open.

Our internal self-guidance, coupled with our intention to pursue higher levels of consciousness, in exactly the perfect way for each of us, allows us to receive and perfectly integrate the information contained in each message.

So then, OUR responsibility, in the process of Conscious Human Evolution, is to be open to all information that is coming through, and learn what we will need to *know* as humanity evolves. This is not to say we must accept or believe everything that is being brought through, or even that which has survived throughout the millennium, but we are responsible to use discernment to determine what resonates with our vibration and what does not.

Each of us may resonate with different truths, but what is significant to note is that those who have chosen to take part in the Ascension process all share a common goal and purpose. The difference lies in the fact that we do not all take the same route. The latest ideas are ours to relish. We can embrace what has never been achieved and know that we are laying the groundwork for all of us to rise above the current situation.

When we acknowledge the selfless contribution we have made in the process, we begin to realize the greatness in ourselves and all those of us who are willing to step into the unknown.

We are Our Own Spiritual Teachers

Those of us who embark on a spiritual journey often have teachers, take classes, go to seminars, and learn various techniques, which have helped in facilitating our participation in Conscious Human Evolution.

We are moving into the Crystalline Era of our spiritual development. What this means is that everything is changing very rapidly. The Earth, our bodies, and minds are adapting to the next phase of human expansion. Whether or not we choose to participate is irrelevant, because it is a process that involves everyone. Eventually we must experience the transition, transmutation, and transformation of life moving towards a higher consciousness.

There is no one who can tell us exactly how to make the journey, which is part of the beauty of the rite of passage. There are no traditions or handed down ceremonies. Each one of us must learn what steps to take on our own. We are our own spiritual teachers, floating on an iceberg that broke off the glacier, stranded on a desert island in the middle of the ocean, and wandering in an infinite wilderness without a compass. But all is not lost, in fact we are less alone than when we had teachers and gurus telling us what to believe and how to go ahead.

Our teachers were sharing what they learned on their path, but their path is not necessarily ours. They do not always know what is best for us, and despite their loving intentions, they might even be keeping us from finding our own way, something we all must do.

There is only one method for each of us to get off the iceberg, away from the island, and out of the wilderness, and the only being that knows that path is each one of us. Our Higher Self knows how to proceed, how to discover answers to the unanswerable, how to find our way when impossibly lost, and how to move from hopelessness to bliss.

There is no New Age pill.

When we listen to the guidance that is our birthright, we begin to understand that we have all the wisdom we require. This does not mean that we turn our backs on the world, it means being an observer and an onlooker. We will not gain wisdom from the goings on of others, but instead from quieting our minds and listening to the dialogue going on between us and our Higher Self.

Everything that is happening right now in our lives has a message for us, a lesson to show us whether we are making useful decisions or those that will cause us to meet resistance. What we can learn from others, are tools to make our journey easier. Whether it be meditation, Yoga, Reiki, dowsing, or crystals, to name a few and there are many more, if we feel drawn to learning or participating in one of these areas, it is meant for us, to make the process easier.

Look within.

There is no one else that can make the journey of Conscious Human Evolution for us. There is no New Age Pill that we can take and suddenly be in Nirvana. We are our own teacher when it comes to our spiritual growth. If we follow someone else, we may realize that we must find our way back on our own and end up where we began. When we stop for a moment, begin a dialogue with ourselves, and keep it going we find that the answers to our questions are there for us and always have been.

Observations of the Masters

When I was a young child, I had an image of a group of *beings* sitting in a glass observation booth, looking down upon life, and watching us as we continued through our days. I never thought it particularly strange that they were there, it seemed so natural to me.

When I glanced up at them, there appeared to be some who were quite busy at work, but always there were those doing nothing but watching. I did not know then what I know now, that they were Angelic guides and Masters, monitoring our daily lives until the time came when we could join them etherically.

As I grew older, I stopped thinking about them, replacing them with more rational thoughts. Even though only a faint memory remained, they continued to watch me until the time came when I would once again remember they were there. It is not acknowledged by many that this is happening, because it is not visible to the naked eye. I put the memory aside until I became aware again that things that are real are visible in other ways.

As Masters, we can assist these loving, *Living Beings* with our intention to move forward in the Ascension process. When we choose to become Enlightened, we join them. We too become the observers, watching the goings-on of life. By perfecting our ability to remain connected yet not participating, we strengthen our purpose, which is to live on Earth today, while inhabiting a new vibrational reality that has been created by those of us who have chosen a heart-centered, love-based approach to living.

As we practice observing others, living through happiness, tragedy, growth, and even death, we perfect our ability to remain energetically connected, yet not affected. In other words, we only allow events, emotions, influences, and all other aspects of life into our reality if their vibration is as high or higher, as our own.

Anything that vibrates lower, we observe, but not embrace, and certainly not integrate into our energy body. This might seem selfish to some; however, our duty is to keep our vibration at the highest level possible. Allowing lower vibrating energies to affect us is not helping anyone, in fact quite the opposite. It is our responsibility to hold the Light.

Be transparent.

By remaining at this higher level of consciousness we have ascended into The New Era, a higher reality right here on Earth. Those of us who have chosen to be Masters in this lifetime are living in a world where life is good, all is well, peace and happiness abound, and prosperity and abundance are part of our everyday existence.

We are living side-by-side with the part of humanity still clinging to the old ways, the struggle, the doubt, and belief that miracles do not happen anymore. We know that we were once in the same place that they are, and that they must find their way just as we did. What we *can* do is shine our Light as bright as possible, to light the path for them.

We have ascended and accomplished our goal of creating a new reality here on Earth. This is not to say that we cannot improve, quite the opposite, this is only the first step and the first major recognizable accomplishment, but it is especially important because it is real, as real as our old reality.

We in The New Era, live each day in harmony, experiencing synchronicity, guided by our feelings and intuition, tinged with grace. It is a mystical, magical life that exists, and is taking place here and now.

We travel etherically, communicate telepathically, receive confirmation of positive thoughts from Violet orbs that we can see with the naked eye, and communicate with beings from other dimensions, all in a day's work. It is truly a wonderfully fascinating time, with fresh discoveries surfacing daily.

The vibrational messages of ancient archeological sites are being reintroduced into our conscious awareness. The molecules in the melting water of polar ice caps are returning to the sea, then evaporating into the air, raining down upon us, and ending up in the water we drink, bringing ancient knowledge and wisdom into our cells.

Messages are left for us, not on sticky notes, but with crop circles in the very fields of grain from which we make bread, our basic food. We do not know exactly what the messages mean, but we do know how we feel when we look at the designs carved into the surface of the Earth, and we also know we will never be the same after visiting one. Those who watched me as a child, were waiting for me to join them so I could observe those around me in the grand, fractal universe in which we find ourselves.

Dimensions

Conscious Human Evolution means becoming aware of our own multi-dimensionality. Although we might be able to conceive of other dimensions, it is sometimes beyond our ability as rational creatures to envision or understand dimensions that are outside of our ordinary reality.

A dimension is a point of view.

A dimension is a vibration, and when we resonate with a vibration, we can claim it as part of our reality. As we ensure our thoughts and actions are of the highest caliber, we must also go farther in the process by releasing sub-conscious lower vibrating energies and thought forms we brought into this lifetime.

Once we release the lower energies, we experience a shift and we are different than we were previously, because we have entered another sub-dimension. Our thoughts become brighter, we hold more Light, and our vibration is altered.

As we move from one place in consciousness to another, we create a new, subtly unique dimension, and we begin to feel differently. We cannot enter a state of consciousness, unless we resonate with it. Therefore, we can safely say that a dimension is a *point of view*.

We use the terms higher and lower, but in truth we are only occupying one unique point or coordinate at a time. We cannot define this point by any adjective that implies duality, since it is only a point. That is what we have been allotted, one tiny dot in the entire scheme of creation, but from that point we can expand infinitely outward, or inward, while still being securely anchored.

Know Thyself

We are all familiar with the ancient phrase, spoken more than a thousand years ago, but the profoundness of the words *know thyself*, is a key element in the Ascension process. *Knowing* ourselves is more than deciding what kind of ice cream we prefer, or even what is our astrological sign, instead, it is the deep remembering of what has been forgotten, but not lost.

As multi-dimensional beings, fragmented throughout creation, our task in this lifetime is to integrate as many of the fragments of ourselves into a unified, new, and improved version. We call this the Ascension Process, and it is happening right now.

Many of us are aware that there is a part of us that knows everything, and that we have experienced other lifetimes, dimensions, and other forms of existence. In addition, that *knowing* includes an unending source of wisdom at our disposal.

We are currently fine-tuning the process of tapping into this divine encyclopedic treasury. This is where *Know Thyself* comes in, as we are fulfilling our purpose for this incarnation.

We must *look within*, to find what is stored in our Sacred Mind, the vault that holds all our treasures. The key to unlock the door is our spiritual journey. It is uniquely our own. It is ongoing, seasoned with Love, giving us the courage and strength to pursue our highest possibilities. Once the journey begins, it becomes our primary purpose and focus, filling up the spaces surrounding our everyday activities.

When we become still, and listen, in the quiet, between breaths, and in the place that is not waking and neither sleep, we find the wisdom of our Soul Self. The voice of guidance in our minds, speaks to us throughout the day, and even in our dreams. When we are unsure of what to do, we can stop and listen for the answers we are looking for. As we accept this guidance, our life will flow seamlessly and gracefully. *Know thyself*, and the miracle that we all are.

A Message from St. Germain

Beloved ones, use the Violet Flame to transmute and clear all things, both big and small, that are not of the highest order. Whenever you have a thought or pull up a memory, which does not feel good to you, cleanse it with the Violet Flame. Do this right away when you have the thought or remember an unpleasant time in your life.

Clear all discordant energies from the event or thought and visualize and imagine the best possible outcome. You will then be free of those thought forms and past event that no longer serve you.

Nothing is too small or insignificant for this process, because many small things add up to something larger. Before you know it, you are lighter and have made progress in your journey to the higher realms.

The Violet Flame is my gift to you, dear ones, use it often. I am with you always.

Saint Germain…

About the Author

Wendy Ann Zellea is an Ascension Messenger and Luminary.

She is the author of six metaphysical books and numerous inspirational articles. She presents esoteric concepts in a clear writing style for a wide audience.

Her work focuses upon bringing through information, from the Higher Realms, for those of us living in the New Era.

Wendy has been a college English instructor, musician, singer and composer, and IT Professional.

More Books by Wendy Ann Zellea

- Ascension Messages From the Higher Realms - *The Process of Conscious Human Evolution*
- My Way Around - *Journeying the Infinite Spiral of Life*
- SAVING ATLANTIS - *A Mystical, Modern Myth*
- Being a Master in the New Era - *Integrating the Codes of Ascension*
- Life is Good, All is Well - *Everything is Vibration*
- Do You Want to Be Happy NOW?

AscensionMessages.com
AnEnlightenedAuthor.com
Wendy@AnEnlightenedAuthor.com

And So It Is…

The End